The

Recollections

of

Mr. A. Prentice (Prent) Kenyon

U. S. Naval Institute
Annapolis, Maryland
1973

Preface

This manuscript is the result of a series of interviews with Mr. A. Prentice (Prent) Kenyon at his office in Ballston Tower #1, Arlington, Virginia. All the interviews were conducted by John T. Mason, Jr., Director of the Oral History program for the U. S. Naval Institute, and cover a period of time extending from November 6, 1972 to March 1, 1973.

Mr. Kenyon retired on March 31, 1973 after serving the Navy since 1941, first as a Reserve Officer and later as a civil servant. Most of the period was spent in BuPers and at the time of his retirement there he held the most senior civil service position in the Navy. Vice Admiral Cagle, with whom Mr. Kenyon worked very closely since 1971, terms him "a legendary figure....a walking history book with regard to training."

The memoir is a comprehensive treatise on education, training and related matters in the U. S. Navy and should prove of much value to those who are interested in these areas.

Minor corrections and emendations were made by Mr. Kenyon to the original transcript. The entire manuscript has been re-typed. The reader is reminded of course that the text as it stands is essentially a record of the spoken word.

A comprehensive subject index has been added for the convenience of the reader.

DECLARATION OF TRUST

The undersigned does hereby appoint and designate as his (her) Trustee herein, the Secretary-Treasurer and Publisher of the United States Naval Institute to perform and discharge the following duties, powers, and privileges in connection with the possession and use of a certain taped interview between the undersigned and the Oral History Department of the United States Naval Institute.

1. Classification of Transcript.

(X)a. If classified OPEN, the transcript(s) may be read or the recording(s) audited by the qualified personnel upon presentation of proper credentials, as determined by the Secretary-Treasurer of the U. S. Naval Institute.

( )b. If classified PERMISSION REQUIRED TO CITE OR QUOTE, the user will be required to obtain permission in writing from the interviewee prior to quoting or citing from either the transcript(s) or the recording(s).

( )c. If classified PERMISSION REQUIRED, permission must be obtained in writing from the interviewee before the transcribed interview(s) can be examined or the tape recording(s) audited.

( )d. If classified CLOSED, the transcribed interview(s) and the tape recording(s) will be sealed until a time specified by the interviewee. This may be until the death of the interviewee or for any specified number of years.

2. It is expressly understood that in giving this authorization, I am in no way precluded from placing such restrictions as I may desire upon use of the interview at any time during my lifetime, nor does this authorization in any way affect my rights to the copyright of my literary expressions that may be contained in the interview.

Witness my hand and seal this 23rd day of March 1973.

Albert Prentice Kenyon

I hereby accept and consent to the foregoing Declaration of Trust and the powers therein conferred upon me as Trustee:

R. T. E. Bowler Jr.

Kenyon 1 - 1

Interview No. 1 with Mr. Prent Kenyon

Place: His office in Arlington, Virginia

Date: Monday afternoon, 6 November 1972

Subject: Biography

By: John T. Mason, Jr.

Q: I'm delighted, Sir, that you have consented to do this series on naval personnel matters and naval education. It gives promise of being a very enlightening series and a very useful one. I wonder if you'd begin by telling me a little about your own personal background, your educational background, your early interest in naval service, and government service, as such?

Mr. K.: I went to college in Milton, Wisconsin, in 1925 and graduated from there in 1929, and went to teach school in northern Illinois.

Q: Where in Illinois?

Mr. K.: In Chadwick, which is about 65 miles straight west of Rockford. It was just about the beginning of the Great Depression in 1929, so school teachers were in difficult circumstances in those days. It was difficult to find a job and difficult to hold a job.

Q: And salaries were uncertain?

Mr. K.: Salaries were insignificant! Then I went back to Columbia, went to Columbia University for four summers from

1933 to 1936.

Q: What school there were you enrolled in?

Mr. K.: Teachers College. I got my master's degree in 1936, and was still teaching school in Illinois until 1937.

Q: Still in Chadwick?

Mr. K.: Still in Chadwick. In 1937 I moved to Westerly, Rhode Island, where I was born, and taught school in the senior high school there, teaching physics and mathematics. When the war started in 1941, I finished out that year, then joined the Navy by asking the Navy in Boston did they have any use for a school teacher. They said yes, we can use a school teacher, sign here. So I signed, and the day school was out, on the 19th of June, I went home and my orders were there, so I went up to Boston, filled out some more papers, and took a physical, and bought a uniform and with that I was in the Navy.

My first duty station was a school called the Harbor Defense School, which was about to be located on Fishers Island, New York, which is off the coast of Connecticut at the mouth of the Thames River. I went on a cold, rainy, Sunday afternoon over to my first duty station in an Army small vessel. I left New London and went over to Fishers Island, got off there, and wandered up to the Army headquarters, the Provost's office, and I said, "Where do I find the Harbor Defense School?" The Army people sitting around there looked at each other and finally one said, "Oh, that's that new thing up at the other end of the island. Get in the jeep and I'll take you up there."

So I got in the jeep and we went about seven miles up to the east end of the island. I got out of the jeep and was met by a warrant officer who was the sole Navy individual on the establishment.

Q: He was the school!

Mr. K.: He was the whole school. It turned out later that there were two more officers, both of whom were lieutenants and who were in the process of having an argument with each other as to who was senior. They were not living at the school which, it turned out, was also located in what was the Fishers Island Country Club that the Navy had taken over from the wealthy people from New York City as a site for this school. I found a place to sleep in the building which resembled a hotel and became a student, first, of the school and pretty soon was elevated to the staff in an administrative capacity.

Q: By this time the students had to flock in?

Mr. K.: Soon some further staff members had shown up. They had been through the sonar school in Key West. Our school was to teach underwater detection devices, various kinds of devices, underwater magnetic loops and what the British call an azimuth were among the tools that we had, and some sonar buoys put out in the harbors and that kind of thing.

I stayed there until October of 1943.

Q: You stayed two years then?

Mr. K.: Well, I went there in June of 1942 and left there in October of 1943, at which time I received orders to the Bureau of Naval Personnel to replace an officer who was concerned with harbor defense schools and harbor entrance control posts training, sonar training, and various other kinds of training of a like nature.

Q: May I ask you one more question about the school? During your period there, approximately how many men passed through, how many men were trained there?

Mr. K.: I would say on the order of perhaps 700 or 800 while I was there. They went to all parts of the world to take up duties in Harbor entrance control posts at various places like the Hawaiian Islands and the Philippines and some of the European ports where they were assigned, and Africa also, to occupy harbor defense kinds of duty stations.

Q: This was more or less pioneering, wasn't it? We hadn't done very much in this area?

Mr. K.: We hadn't done enough, obviously, because the Pearl Harbor situation could have been different had the harbor there been properly protected. They did have some of this type of detection device, but it obviously wasn't sufficient and didn't give them enough warning.

Q: Did you have any officers from the Royal Navy on the staff there at the school?

Mr. K.: Not continously. We did have some contact with the Royal Navy people and we learned a lot from their shipborne azimuth experiences primarily, not from their harbor defense activities. They had a real good capability for detecting submarines from shipboard.

I was with the Bureau of Naval Personnel from there on for the rest of the war.

Q: What rank were you by that time?

Mr. K.: I came into the Navy as a lieutenant, (jg), and when I was in BuPers I got promoted to lieutenant. I seem to have slipped through lieutenant commander pretty fast because by the time the war ended I was a commander. Late in 1945 I had orders to the office of the Chief of Naval Operations, where I was a member of the secretariat of the Training Policy Board, which had been formed by that time due, in some measure any way, to my instigation that there was a need for such an organization. I only spent four months in that occupation, at which time I got orders back to BuPers and then got out of uniform for the first time in July of 1946. I was called back for a short time in 1947, and got out again on the 1st of July 1948, I think it was.

Q: Finally? Out of uniform?

Mr. K.: Finally out of uniform, although I remained a member of the Reserve over the years and put in enough time taking correspondence courses and going to drill so that I finally got retired from the Naval Reserve and now, since I'm old enough, they pay me for being retired from the Naval Reserve.

Q: Sir, would you mind harking back and telling me something about that Training Policy Board, which you inspired them to set up immediately after the war? What was its scope? What was its intention?

Mr. K.: During the war it was obvious that fragmentation of various sorts had set in as far as the training establishment was concerned. One of the first jobs that our group had when I came into BuPers--it had been called the Bureau of Navigation but was now the Bureau of Naval Personnel--was to go up and down the east and west coasts to take an accounting of all the different training activities or courses that had sprung up. Each of the Naval District commandants had undertaken his own training program and there wasn't even any record anywhere at that time of how many courses, what duplication there might be, and so on and so forth.

One of our functions was to collect all of these things and get them under at least some kind of knowledgeable guidance.

Q: To bring order out of a certain amount of chaos!

Mr. K.: Right. Admiral King recognized this difficulty in 1941 and directed that the Bureau of Naval Personnel take cognizance of all training in the Navy. The Bureau endeavored to do this, but ran into some administrative difficulty, particularly with regard to who was in charge of amphibious training. They took time out to inquire from ComInch as to whether he meant really that the Bureau was to take over amphibious training or not.

Q: And would he back them if they did?

Mr. K.: Well, that was by implication, but you remember that at that time there was ComInch and there was CNO, and ComInch was supposed to be, in somebodys' minds anyway, in charge of the fleet and CNO was in charge of the shore establishment. Somehow or other amphibious got to be a shore establishment kind of operation and CNO said, No, keep your fingers off of amphibious. Admiral King was both ComInch and CNO, but their staffs didn't always see alike.

So the Bureau of Naval Personnel was trying manfully to take over all of these things without really knowing what was going on in various places.

Q: I suppose the proliferation was due to war time expediency, wasn't it?

Mr. K.: Expediency. Everybody going and doing what they thought was the thing to do under the circumstances. In the meantime, the submarine threat was becoming more and more serious, so Admiral King obviously, from the papers that are still extant, became impatient with the situation and said, I'm going to create two fleet training commands, which were called CotLant and CotPac, Commander Operational Training, Atlantic, and Pacific. He specifically put certain activities under those two fleet type commanders. Among them were the sonar schools, called sound schools, one of which was at Key West and one in San Diego, which had sprung up as fleet schools, perhaps in the late 1930s. And another one was the motor torpedo boat training center from which John F. Kennedy came, as a matter of interest, which was at Melville, Rhode Island.

There were about four or five different types of schools that he specifically assigned to CotLant and CotPac.

Q: And this was by fiat?

Mr. K.: By fiat by a letter. This, in effect, then said to the Bureau of Naval Personnel, forget about those things which are associated primarily with fleet things, as far as you're concerned. However, you have a responsibility because you're the fellow that's going to have to supply the manpower and the money to run these schools.

Q: This was a difficult situation for the Bureau, wasn't it?

Mr. K.: Right. When, as I said before, we went up and down the coasts to find out what was going on, we actually created a number of activities like what later became the Fleet Training Center at Boston. The Bureau of Naval Personnel put those activities under CotLant on the east coast and under CotPac on the west coast. In other words, we collected those things that had sprung up overnight and gave them a boss, so to speak, by this means. This was in 1943-44.

Q: Were you running into opposition from the local commanders? The base commanders on the coasts?

Mr. K.: Not really. They had created these schools. They needed some help, and they were anxious to have somebody from Washington who had resources and was able to provide for them and keep them going. They were anxious to make them bigger, of course, in the usual proliferation, but I don't remember any opposition specifically. It was a day when there was great urgency, of course, and Washington was coming out and saying this is the way we'll do it, so all right that's the way we'll do it. Everybody was on the same team, you might say.

Q: How long a period were you out in the field there?

Mr. K.: It extended over a period of a couple of years with different people going to different areas, geographical areas, and looking at different things. For example, the first trip that I made to the west coast was in 1944 to look at the harbor defense schools, the Harbor Entrance Control Posts (HECPs), the sonar schools, and that sort of thing, so as to make sure we were aware of all that was going on and to collect them all together in such a way as to put them under a boss in some way. So it was over a protracted period.

Q: And I suppose meanwhile others were springing up?

Mr. K.: Well, by this time we had a fair control over the situation. In other words, we now had an office. The Chief of Naval Personnel had not had any real training office before World War II came along. Training at that time was divided into two kinds, officer training and enlisted training. Therefore, there was an office which consisted of perhaps one or two officers only who were located in the officer detailing room, and another set of officers were in the enlisted detailing group, and they constituted the training effort, you might say, of the Bureau of Naval Personnel of that day.

Now, when World War II came along and a management study was made by Booz, Frye, Allen and Hamilton, one of the things that they came up with was that there ought to be what amounted to a training division in the Bureau of Naval Personnel. So it came about and was in being when I arrived on the scene. That is, the training organization had been created.

One of the other things that Booz, Frye, Allen and Hamileton, found out was that there ought to be more kinds of training than just officer and enlisted training. They created a new kind of training, a new name, operational training. This was the group in which I was assigned, and this included those things which were of an operational nature, which might include both officers and enlisted men.

Q: Did this pertain to new ordnance that was coming out?

Mr. K.: Yes, it could, but it was more apt to be in things like the CIC or the sonar shack where you required the services of several different types of specialization and maybe officers and enlisted men in the same occupational specialty, you might say.

Q: I was thinking of such things as radar. I mean when the Washington was getting commissioned and getting ready to go to Europe radar was installed and there had to be a certain amount of training for the men who were to operate it.

Mr. K.: In the case of radar, you would have put your people through the radio technicians' school of that day at what you might consider the elementary level where they learned what an electron was and which way it was supposed to go and which wire to hook where and so on. Then you would send them into an operational type of school where they learned, together with others, to operate as a team and to work in a maintenance situation as a team also. The operational type of school included such things as I've already mentioned-- the harbor defense, the fleet-type activities, sonar, CIC, anti-air warfare training, deep-sea diving, and all that kind of thing which didn't fit neatly into what we used to call, and still do call, rate training. In other words, the individual is not training to get a rating, he is training as a specialist.

Q: What about communications, as such?

Mr. K.: Well, radioman was a type of training but it was usually, and still is today, handled as a function of enlisted personnel rate training. In other words, they learned to operate radio devices and maintain radio devices for communications. But on a broader scale, yes, you would have communications courses at fleet training centers, where people who were already assigned to a ship would have the opportunity to go to that fleet training center and practice their communications and keep their hands in by getting a refresher course. Even today we have radioman courses, refresher courses, in fleet training centers ashore.

Q: Well, you stepped into the midst of that when you came to the Bureau?

Mr. K.: Right. And so, having gone through this during World War II, as World War II was coming to and end in

1945, it was evident to some of us that there ought to be some way of pulling together the total training of the Navy. And so we proposed in 1945--I've got an excerpt from it around here somewhere.

Q: And here is the excerpt. What is the date?

Mr. K.: This is an excerpt from a BuPers memo to the Assistant Chief of Staff, Readiness, in the office of ComInch, dated October 1945:

> "Because the shore establishment should and does exist for the benefit of the forces afloat, I am taking this opportunity of proposing for your consideration the following plan which I believe will most effectively meet the needs of the Fleet with a minimum use of funds and personnel and with the least amount of duplication of effort.
>
> 1. Establish within the office of CNO a single agency responsible for the determination, control, and promulgation of over-all training policy. This agency should be staffed with personnel representing each fundamental type of training and should likewise be represented by senior officers attached to fleet units. This central agency would thus be enabled to learn the needs of the fleets, function as a central controlling agency in the determination of policy, and to direct the implementation of the determined policies.

2. Responsibility for the control of implementation of shore-based training policies must likewise be vested in a single agency for most effective results. Because the over-all cognizance of personnel rests with BuPers, this Bureau is logically best fitted to assume the centralized implementation of all shore-based training. This would provide a single agency which at all times would possess a complete picture of shore-based training. This single implementing agency would obtain policy approval of training programs from the central policy control agency and would seek advice as necessary from the material bureaus and other technical agencies."

Q: So that was the charter for it?

Mr. K.: This resulted in a consideration by the Chief of Naval Operations. As s result a training policy board was created 16 November 1945 by Admiral E. J. King. This board was created in OpNav to coordinate and exercise general review functions over policies affecting the Navy's training activities to the end that an adequate state of training is attained and maintained without duplication of effort. Establishment of this board was approved by James V. Forrestal, SecNav, and the first senior member was Rear Admiral Jerauld Wright, who later became CincLantFlt.

Q: Was there any influence--was the board influenced in any way by the plans which were then under way for reducing the size of the Navy? Did that have any bearing on the whole subject?

Mr. K.: Yes, I'm sure there was because in that day the name of the game was to find a way to operate a peacetime Navy with reduced resources. One of the things that was given consideration at that time was the elimination of CotLant and CotPac as fleet commanders and the reinstitution of shore-based training, except for flight training, under the Chief of Naval Personnel. However, this was not to be. The policy board decided in a rather controversial session that the fleet training commanders would remain, they would have their names changed, and they would be called Commanders, Training Command, Atlantic, and Pacific, which they still retain as their titles today.

Q: What was the controversy within the board, as they considered this subject?

Mr. K.: The different of opinion was primarily one of whether or not the fleet's interest in training could be adequately taken care of by the Bureau of Naval Personnel and the shore establishment without having some direct representation by the fleet.

Q: Were you called upon to give your advice in this session?

Mr. K.: Yes. I had a part in it as a member of the Board's secretariat, but I didn't have much choice as far as the decision was concerned.

Q: What was your stance?

Mr. K.: I thought that the shore establishment in the reduced Navy would be viable, as we said in this previous letter to ComInch, if the entire implementation of training in the shore establishment were to be under one head, and that logically should be BuPers.

THE FORMATIVE YEARS

At this point it might be well to review briefly the earlier history of training in the Navy. The training conducted by the Navy up until the early twentieth century was primarily accomplished aboard ship. It was the principle of the leaders of the Navy at that time that this was the best way to train people. Schools ashore generally were not needed. Of course, the Naval Academy came along in 1845 and a Naval War College in 1881, and the Navy recognized the value of graduate education by the creation of the postgraduate school in Annapolis in 1909. But, in general, training took place aboard ship.

Q: This was certainly in the day of the sailing ship when everything was uncomplicated, wasn't it?

Mr. K.: Yes, in the day of the sailing ship and later in the day of steam. In the early days, the practice was to bring young men into some location--Newport was the primary location--where they were given a short period on shore, but most of their training took place actually in the ships of the Navy. What little education and training that existed prior to World War II was generally administered by the Bureau of Navigation (later changed to the Bureau of Naval Personnel). Annual reports of the Bureau of Navigation, some date back as far as 1890, are in existence. There was very little attention to training in the early years--only a few paragraphs among 112 pages in the 1890 report for example. The stationary training ships at Newport, (because the Richmond replaced the New Hampshire that year) were mentioned. In this connection, it is interesting to note that the first billeting of students ashore, first in tents, later in a gymnasium and still later in a Naval War College building, resulted because typhoid fever made its appearance on the stationary ship New Hampshire. Medical officers at the station considered it unwise to requarter the students on the New Hampshire. However, training was still accomplished on the ship.

Q: May I ask, was our method of training aboard ship on a par with what the Royal Navy did and the French Navy and the other important ones?

Mr. K.: I really don't know about that. I am sure the U. S. Navy borrowed many things from the Royal Navy and had much contact with the Royal Navy in those days.

The 1890 report mentioned gunnery schools at Washington and Newport in one paragraph but no other schools are mentioned. With regard to apprenticeship training aboard ship, a couple of paragraphs seem worthy of note in the lithe of current Navy problems: "The period of instruction in the cruising training ships has been increased to one year with beneficial results. Large numbers of boys present themselves for enlistment as apprentices, but many are rejected for physical disqualifications and some of those accepted fail to report. The average number of enlisted falls below the number allowed by law, and the gain to the service has not been encouraging."

"Many boys enter the Navy for the novelty of the life of which they soon tire and many are entered by their parents apparently with a view to having their boys educated and disciplined before putting them to other work."

Two decades later training of enlisted men emcompassed four pages of the fifty-four page report and postgraduate courses in engineering and special classes in ordnance covered 1/2 a page. By 1920 the Navy had four recruit training stations and fifty-four trade schools showed in the report covering 31 specializations, including musicians. There were actually two music schools vice the one the Navy has today. The student population on 30 June 1920 was 5,802. This seems like a large number, which undoubtedly reflected the influence of World War I.

And so it went with training specialties gradually

showing on the scene, but only in World War II was there a rapid rise in training effort which generally has continued to increase proportionately since that time.

Q: May I interrupt with a question? Prior to World War II just before World War II and during the decade of the 30s when the depression was a very important element in our national life, I am told that enlistments in the Navy were men of real education very often and high standards, men who could not find jobs in private life and who came into the Navy. In your knowledge of the whole situation, do you see this reflected in any way in Navy training?

Mr. K.: I am not prepared to speak as to why they came in, but a lot of my early associates in the Navy came in directly from college. I always thought they came because they were forward looking and saw the handwriting on the wall and wanted to get in while the getting was good. One of the first officer supervisors that I had in the Bureau of Naval Personnel was a graduate of the NROTC program about 1939, for example, and he was a very smart, well educated young man. So a lot of good people were coming into the Navy, for whatever reason, in the late 1930s.

At this point it may be useful to review the activities of Naval education and training in the various wars. In 1955 the President's Commission on Veterans Pensions requested DOD to make a factual, historical study of the conditions of military life, including education and training aspects. Accordingly, considerable data covering the wars between the Civil War and the 1955 era was collected and tabulated. Some excerpts are paraphrased as follows:

In the Civil War recruit training, conducted principally on board ship, had the basic purposes, first to indoctrinate the recruit in military discipline, courtesy and care of clothing and equipment, and second to teach the rudiments of combat at sea. Advanced individual and unit training was conducted on ships of the fleet and responsibility for training rested almost completely with the operating forces.

Little change was found in recruit training in the war with Spain. Also the vast majority of personnel were trained aboard ship. However, in this period Naval apprentices, who were boys between the ages of 16 and 18, were given a 5-6 month course of instruction at Newport, Rhode Island. In addition to general training and seamanship, gunnery, gymnastics, and care of clothing and equipment, the apprentices were schooled in reading, writing and arithmetic.

By the time of the start of World War I the Navy's four training stations offered a recruit-type training over periods of 3-6 months. The emphasis still remained on training aboard ship, but during World War I Navy training was provided in Navy service schools, civilian education institutions and industrial plants. Included among the civilian institutions were Harvard, Columbia and Dunwoody Industrial Institute, Minneapolis, Minnesota.

While the shore based training effort gradually increased between the two world wars, it was not until World War II that training came into its own. Recruit training was the same as previously, except that such specializations as lookout recognition, telephone talking, fire fighting and chemical warfare were newly added subject matter areas. The length of training varied from three weeks to twelve weeks depending on how fast men were needed afloat as several hundreds of thousands poured into the Navy.

For the first time, extensive attention was given to officer indoctrination. The Naval Academy graduations were speeded up as were also the NROTC courses, the first units of which had been established in 1926. These two sources were far from sufficient to supply the need, so many thousands of officers were commissioned directly from civilian status. This was a fortunate event for Navy education and training since many of these were school teachers or administrators and many of them stayed on in the Navy after World War II to provide a substantive pedagogical base which to this day exerts a strong influence on Navy training efforts.

Time and energy do not permit an elaboration of training effort to the extent it deserves in World War II and the decade thereafter, including the Korean Conflict. Suffice it to say, whereas in World War I only 9.4% of Navy personnel received specialized training in schools ashore, 80.2% received such training in World War II. The percentages recorded for the Korean Incident and for the more peaceful 1955 era were 68.3 and 60.9, respectively.

This same DOD report shows a trend that is significant for education and training. About 23% of personnel school trained in World War I were enrolled in soft skill schools such as administrative and clerical. By World War II this percentage had dropped to about 3%, showing that the preponderance of training was veering toward the more technical hardware and militarily oriented skills, giving increased impetus to school training on the beach.

Q: This indicates then, does it not, that the complexity of the training need was on the increase?

Mr. K.: Yes, that is true. We had by that time radar, for example. It had been invented and a lot of technical equipment was being put on new ships as they were being rapidly built. There was a need for training hundreds of thousands of enlisted personnel through recruit and technical training and officers through officer indoctrination and officer training. All of these things made for a very rapid growth in the effort of Navy training. The need has grown ever since.

I would illustrate the reason for this increase by reference to a graph created by Harold F. Clark and Harold S. Sloan in their little book published by Teachers College, Columbia University in 1964 called <u>Classrooms in the Mili-</u>

tary. We have often used this thesis in our arguments in defense of the need to put a higher proportion of Navy people through schools.

Even this past year we have been endeavoring to defend the fact that a higher proportion of Navy end strength is now in education and training programs in comparison with a period as recently in the past as 1965. The chart referred to traces the creation of Navy training activities from the advent of the Naval Academy in 1845 up to 1960 in relationship to the expenditure by the U. S. for research and development. The R&D expenditure rises only slightly from practically zero in 1860 up to less then $1 billion in 1940. From that time and for the next two decades, R&D expenditures skyrocketed up to more then $13 billion by 1960. In this period came such training demanding events as helicopters, jet airplanes, atomic and nuclear power and weapons, computers, guided missiles, transistors, Sputnik and U. S. satellite and moon excursions.

Q: Is it any wonder then that the need for training has expanded many fold since 1940 and is still rising?

Mr. K.: No, it is completely understandable. This is particularly true when one considers that in addition to the continuing technological development, the Navy, along with society in general, has found it necessary through education and training to deal with such sociological phenomena as race relations, drug and alcohol abuse, human resources management and enlistment and re-enlistment incentives. Now that the Navy faces the era of the zero draft, it is necessary to look forward to a continually increasing demand for education and training as an incentive to meet the competition for manpower which the civilian economy will exert.

Q: Now that you have brought us up to the World War II era, would you like to go back to a further discussion of the education and training organization which came into being after World War II?

ORGANIZATION FOR NAVY TRAINING

Mr. K.: Yes, sir. As I have previously mentioned, the Chief of Naval Operations Training Policy Board came into existence in the late months of 1945. The first four months of 1946 were spent in arduous board discussions, primarily regarding Navy training organization. The Secretariat and most of the board favored adoption of the plan proposed by BUPERS--a CNO policy office and the CNP as the implementing agency. But the Air contingent rebelled and at one notorious board session threatened to desert the Navy and become aligned with the then newly established U. S. Air Force. Accordingly, the matter was elevated to higher levels.

ADM Radford who was the OP-05, the DCNO (Air)--and ADM Denfeld who was then OP-01--the DCNO (Manpower) discussed the matter, but failed to reach agreement so the issue was discussed with the VCNO, ADM Ramsay late one afternoon. ADM Ramsay declined to referee the argument and told ADM Radford and Denfeld to go away and settle their problem themselves.

RADM Thomas L. Sprague who was the Deputy Chief of Naval Personnel and an aviation officer took a personal interest in this matter. I suspect that ADM Radford exerted some influence in promoting ADM Sprague's interest. Anyway, he appeared on the scene one day in the Training Policy Board Secretariat office with a draft of a directive designed to define the responsibilities for Navy training. This was issued as a CNO directive signed on 17 April 1946 by ADM Chester W. Nimitz who was then the CNO. It is interesting to note that the CNO directive was identified by Pers-1-dy because Admiral Sprague insisted it should bear the symbol of the BUPERS Deputy Chief who created it and thus settled "for all time" the dispute regarding Navy training responsibility.

The 17 April 1946 directive really defined the status quo. This stated briefly that aviation training was a responsibility of DCNO (Air); Medical training was the responsibility of the Chief of BUMED; OP-03, the DCNO for Readiness, was responsible for training afloat; and all other training--basic, technical, etc.--was the responsivility of BUPERS. This remained the basic guidance for training responsibility for many years. It was later incorporated, virtually unchanged, into the Basic Naval

Establishment Plan--a document issued annually. This plan was later discontinued and with it went the last official statement, in any one document, of the assignment of training responsibilities. The latest edition of Navy Regs assigned responsibility for training, except for Medical training, to BUPERS, "except as otherwise assigned". No document was known to exist, however, which assigned training responsibility otherwise.

Q: You mentioned the responsibility for training being identified in the Navy Regulations. How frequently were those regulations pertaining to that subject upgraded?

Mr. K.: The one that was extant at that time was the 1920 edition. The regulations were revised, but not completely overhauled except at very infrequent periods. Recent actions in 1971 and 1972 resulting from the Cagle Board may be said to have changed all this, but that is another story for later.

There was another important issue that needed resolution by the Board: What to do with COTLANT/PAC? This issue was finally resolved in a high level meeting chaired by the senior member of the Training Policy Board--ADM Wright's successor--and attended by ADM William Fechteler, then the CNP, I think, ADM James L. Holloway, Jr. and other high ranking officers whose names I have forgotten. There was much sentiment in favor of abolishing the COTS and much discussion in this vein. The final outcome, however, was a decision to retain the Commands, but change their names to Commander, Training Command, Atlantic/Pacific. We were then back to a World War II organization and there the Navy has stayed for about 25 years.

Q: Did this seem a rational solution to the problem at the time or was it largely reflecting the influence of rather powerful figures like ADM Radford?

Mr. K.: In my opinion if reflected the influence of powerful figures who prescribed the destiny of the organization for Navy training which has endured over the past quarter century. The Training Policy Board lingered on for a number of years but became increasingly inactive. I was ordered back to BUPERS--still in uniform--about April 1946. This time I was the Assistant Head of the Operational Training Section which, at about that time, because of the conflict with training afloat in the operating forces, was changed in name to the Functional Training Section.

The demise of the Training Policy Board left a vacuum in OPNAV regarding education and training, except for Aviation training. This gave Aviation training a powerful position with a strong organization to assure the importance of its position and its prestige. OP-05 and his subordinate offices directed and supported Aviation training at the Washington level. In the field, the Aviation organization had a Vice Admiral as Chief of Naval Air Training (CNATRA) with headquarters at Pensacola and he had four subordinate

Rear Admirals--one each for basic flight training, advanced flight training, technical training and Air Reserve training. It was a powerful organization.

By contrast the BUPERS organization possessed no comparable strong ally within OPNAV and its rank structure was relatively weak. Although responsible for 70/80% of Navy education and training, the program was administered by an organization in BUPERS headed by only one Rear Admiral and that less than 30% of the time--about 9 years out of the nearly 32 years between 1940 and 1972. The record shows that the senior man in the BUPERS training division was a Captain more than 70% of the time.

Q: It would appear then that the BUPERS training organization was undermanned, was it not?

Mr. K.: Yes, particularly from a horsepower point of view. It was necessary for us to enlist the support of the Chief of Naval Personnel himself when we found ourselves in need of flag rank support. In addition to this, the BUPERS training organization sorely missed a focal point in OPNAV, finding itself at the mercy of every OP number who took the time and effort to invent a training requirement. This led in later years to establishment of a committee within OP-03 known as the Standing Committee for Personnel Training and Readiness (SCPTR). This group held periodic meetings and discussed various problems related to training. It served as a sounding board and performed a useful purpose, but possessed little real authority or influence.

In the early years following World War II, there was little dissatisfaction with the Navy's training organization. It weathered the Louis Johnson austerity era and the Korean incident. In 1955, however, during one of those recurring reviews of the Navy's shore establishment designed to curtail it, the Hopwood Board recommended, among many other recommendations that a senior officer be designated as Chief of Naval Training (other-than-Air) and further recommended "that a study be instituted to determine the feasibility of having one training director with deputies for Air and other-than-Air training".

Q: What was the attitude of the Chief of Naval Personnel regarding this recommendation?

Mr. K.: VADM James L. Holloway, Jr., who was then the Chief of Naval Personnel and double hatted as OP-01, resisted strongly this recommendation, but did agree to a compromise which would establish a Commander, Naval Reserve Training Command. This gave birth to the formation of that field command at Omaha, Nebraska. The command was independent and reported directly to CNO, but operated under the management control of BUPERS, which meant really that it received its support and much of its guidance from BUPERS--a combination of Pers-D--the Assistant Chief for Naval Reserve and Pers-C--the Assistant Chief for Education and Training.

All was relatively quiet training organization-wise

until 1961 when President John F. Kennedy visited a Navy ship to, among other things, watch a firing of a Navy guided missile. The missile didn't fire--so all hell broke loose. The Bureau of Weapons was blamed for producing hardware that wouldn't behave properly. BUWEPS held the problem was not with the hardware, but with the training. The solution, BUWEPS said, was to place all weapons training under BUWEPS. This became a major issue which mounted up into OPNAV. A result of this controversy, in which I played a predominant and unpleasant role, was the formation of the Pride Board to decide what should be done to promote better training.

Q: Was that Admiral Mel Pride?

Mr. K.: Yes. The Pride Board was headed by Admiral Alfred M. Pride, USN Retired. I suspect his selection was prompted by some degree of poetic justice, since he was a former Chief of BUWEPS. In 1949, ADM Pride had written: "The writer suggests only what is needed more than anything else in this Navy is some peace and quiet, and suggests, more earnestly, that we just settle down for a while and stop rocking the boat".

In the missile arena, it was obvious by 1961 that ADM Pride's sage words had gone unheeded. The Navy had hastened into the surface to air missile field with vigor. The three Ts--Terrier, Tartar, Talos--were all in being. A principal problem from the trainer's viewpoint was the fact that not only were there several missiles, but there were also several models of each missile. Furthermore, the ambition to get the missiles--launchers, directors, etc. aboard ship was so great that practically no units were being made available as training vehicles. So trainees were being trained by reading pamphlets and charts and the models were changing so fast that no updated manuals or charts were extant. The shining example--not exaggerated-- was there were six or seven different models of the Talos with one each on that same number of ships and when a model was finally made available for training it was unlike any of the other dissimilar models already on ships.

Membership of the Pride Board included RADM F. S. Withington, USN, Retired--another weapons expert--, a future Superintendent of the Postgraduate School and a future Navy Inspector General. RADM P. D. Stroop, then the Chief of BUWEPS, was among those who advised the Pride Board, and there were witnesses from the Army and Air Force and from BUPERS and many other departmental offices, including VADM W. F. Raborn, Jr. of the Special Projects Office. I was one of the witnesses.

Q: Did the Pride Board give consideration to consolidating all of training under a single command?

Mr. K.: Yes. The Pride Board examined the idea of incorporating the operation of all Navy training under a single field command outside of Washington. This idea was discarded as being too disruptive and expensive without sufficient compensating gains at this time. The Board recommended in December 1961: (1) better support at the OPNAV level--by inference, like that given to Air training--and (2) that there be established a focal point for training with OPNAV.

Q: I believe you said earlier that it was the Pride Board that made the point that certain civilian personnel within the Bureau of Naval Personnel were too influential in the development of personnel policies. How did you meet this opposition?

Mr. K.: No, that was VADM Fitzhugh Lee that made that statement. Admiral George Anderson--then the CNO--had convened the Pride Board. He was obviously not pleased with the results thereof and directed OP-03 to make an internal OPNAV study to develop a plan for the formation of a single Navy training command. There is evidence that Admiral Anderson was influenced in this matter somewhat by VADM Fitzhugh Lee who was then CNATRA. While at Memphis, ADM Lee had advanced a plan behind the scenes for amalgamating all training under one command. I don't recall seeing this plan, so it was probably routed by unofficial means. The Cagle Board report does mention such a plan. While he was CNATRA, ADM Lee, apparently in response to a communication from ADM Anderson, advised the CNO in a personal letter that the remainder of training should be organized on the basis of the highly successful Air training organization.

One of the troubles with the BUPERS training organization, ADM Lee said, was that there were too many civilians in Pers-C making decisions that should be made by military professionals. This was not true, but I am sure it was a commonly held conviction by many Navy people not close to the situation. This comment made a sufficient impression on me so that when we reorganized Pers-C in 1965, we assured that a military billet appeared at every point of decision in the new organization structure. I was aware of ADM Lee's comments because it was my task--privilege maybe--to prepare the rebuttal thereto which the Chief of Naval Personnel signed. Later on ADM Lee came into the Bureau of Naval Personnel to help us with a study just before he took over as President of the Naval War College. He and I got much better acquainted at that time, and I am sure that he became convinced and told me so that he recognized when he had more association with BUPERS that we had a real profound kind of job and that he could see why it was that we could not do things as well as the Air training command did, which was a much smaller, narrower field.

Now to continue with the study which Admiral Anderson directed. The CNO directed OP-03 study was headed by then Captain Mason Freeman, later Pers-C, later COMCRUDESPAC and now the Superintendent of the Postgraduate School. So, I refer to this effort as the Freeman Board although its report was never published outside of the Navy Department and it was really an ad hoc group study. I was a member of the study group and furnished some background, but most of the work was done single handed by Mason Freeman.

The Freeman Board which reported in March 1962 devised a plan for amalgamating all Navy training under one head in four phases. The first of these was the establishment of a focal point within OPNAV for all training other than Air. The final phase would have brought Air and non-Air training together as an entity under a single field training commander. OP-03 in his endorsement on the plan recommended consummation of the first phase, but advised delay in effecting the other phases.

Q: What were the other phases? Are you intending to mention them?

Mr. K.: The other phases were by a gradual phasing to create what amounted to a training command in the Atlantic area and a training command in the Pacific area and then later on still to join all of this non-aviation training with Aviation training into a single command.

Q: A gradual means of amalgamating them?

Mr. K.: Right.

Q: In a painless way?

Mr. K.: It would have resulted in, finally, if all four

steps had been taken, having all of training under a single training command, but this was not to be at this time. I well remember a late evening session with Admiral Anderson to discuss this matter. VADM W. R. Smedberg, III, then the Chief of Naval Personnel, Captain A. R. "Tony" Gallaher, then Pers-C and I were present. Captain Freeman and OP-03 and several other high ranking officers were also there as was the VCNO, ADM Claude Ricketts. The discussion was heated with the CNO obviously favoring going further faster, but others including the VCNO cautioning against the disruption and cost of the effort involved--in other words siding with the findings of the Pride Board.

At the conclusion of this lengthy session, ADM Anderson said, in effect, okay, I'll go along with you fellows, but mark my words right here and now, we are going to have a single training command in this Navy, if I am here long enough to bring it about. History records that ADM Anderson left the Navy to become Ambassador to some country before he was able to carry out his threat.

Q: Yes, the Cuban Missile Crisis intervened. I take it, sir, that hopefully you were a part of the consulting staff for these various boards as they came along?

Mr. K.: Yes. I appeared before the Hopwood Board as far back as the 1955 era and represented the Bureau of Naval Personnel's position at that time. I also had many sessions with the Pride Board when they were in the process of their review and deliberations, and I was a member of the Freeman Committee which developed the in-house study. So I have been close to it all the way along.

Q: Again, you have been the continuity for these various boards. I take it that the same personnel did not serve on them?

Mr. K.: That is true. As far as I can remember there was no one on one board that was on any other. Several of the people who were on the Pride Board have just recently retired. These included VADM John Tyree who was later the Navy Inspector General and RADM Marshal E. "Mush" Dornin who was later the Superintendent of the Navy's Postgraduate School. The net result of the Pride and Freeman Board efforts was the establishment of Op-03T, the OPNAV focal point. The remainder of the training organization remained in status quo.

Q: You mentioned one other name here in the outline, Dillon. Was that also a special board?

Mr. K.: The Dillon Board was a group which studied all of Navy organization and in passing they took cognizance of the organization for Navy education and training.

Q: Was this Douglas Dillon?

Mr. K.: No, this was John Dillon who was the Administrative Assistant to the Secretary of the Navy. This was in

Kenyon 1 - 37

1962 and the net result of this board with respect to training was to recommend that the reorganization for training be re-examined after OP-03T had been in position for over a year. This re-examination was accomplished jointly by OP-03T who at that time was RADM E. A. "Count" Ruckner and RADM A. S. "Sandy" Heyward, Jr., who was then the Deputy CNP and an aviation officer who was later CNATRA. I was not present during these negotiations, but a colleague of mine--John Farson--was. He reports that ADM Heyward argued effectively and with obvious success for a continuation of the status quo rather than a decrease in the role played by BUPERS and an increase--East and West--of the role of fleet training commanders regarding shore-based training. The VCNO decided about November 1963 to retain matters in status quo.

Q: Sir, when these boards were considering the organization and the establishment of new policies, did SECDEF have any voice in this? Did he have a representative on the board? Was there any concern by SECDEF about this development within the Navy?

Mr. K.: The Dillon Board was really a SECNAV Board and therefore its recommendations were approved by the Secretary of the Navy. Nowever, in general, the Secretary of Defense was usually on the outside as far as these reorganization studies were concerned. There was no influence from the OSD level on Navy organization for training.

The story of OP-03T, later OP-37, later still OP-01C, is one by itself. Suffice it to say for this record that the idea behind the formation of this OPNAV focal point was a step in the right direction. It has undoubtedly exerted commendable influence, but it had its handicaps. It was essentially a staff office without resource tools, so its influence, especially among OPNAV offices, either senior to it or on an equal level, was exerted, perforce, through persuasion rather than by edict. As was the case in Pers-C, as previously mentioned, there was a tendency to gap the flag billet for long periods of time and in the OPNAV organization even a RADM finds it difficult to gain entree to many decision making arenas. So the impact of OP-03T/OP/37/OP-01C has not been all that it should have been.

This office in the form of OP-01C/OP-14 formed the nucleus for the creation in 1971 of the current OP-099 which is the Cagle Board OPNAV focal point and which will be discussed more fully later.

Interview No. 2 with Mr. Prent Kenyon

Place: Balliston Towers, #1, Arlington, Virginia

Date: Thursday morning, 25 January 1973

Subject: Biography

By: John T. Mason, Jr.

Q: Good to see you this morning, Mr. Kenyon. It's a relatively quiet day and we can accomplish a great deal, I expect. You wanted to continue in accordance with your outline and talk about INSGEN.

Mr. K.: Good morning, Jack.

Between 1963 and the middle of 1970 there were no real outside pressures for reorganization of BuPers training organization, but organizational changes in other areas of the Department were being felt within Pers C. One of these was the creation of a project manager system for weapons development and coordination. The project manager for FBM had been in existence for some years, a surface-to-air missile manager and an ASW czar had now been created, and other project managers for other areas of emphasis were on the horizon.

Accordingly, Rear Admiral Mason Freeman, who was then Pers C, decreed that Pers C should be reorganized so as to reflect among other things this developing pattern related to weapons systems. Accordingly, the first division developed on the new organization chart was one called the Weapons Systems and Fleet Training Division. Other divisions were the Service Schools Training Division, the Officer Education Division, and the General Military Training and Support Division.

As previously noted, another premise was to assure that a military individual was at each decision point in the organization. We also had, by that time, a felt need for a programming office prompted by the increasing acceptance of the so-called resource management system, (RMS). Thus, the problem at hand was a reorganization from two divisions into four, plus a programming staff office. To make matters more complex--

Q: They were complex enough!

Mr. K.: Right--we were intent on changing from a functional organization divided basically on the lines of 1) instructional standards and materials--the what and how of subject matter to be taught, and administration of non-school professional development programs, and 2) management of school facilities, student inputs, staffing, physical facilities, etc. In other words, the why, where, when, and who involved in schoolhouse management. In place of this procedural concept we organized on the basis of weapons systems, types of schools and programs.

This called for a major upheaval, and add to this the problem of distributing equitably the available military and civilian talent in terms of billets and bodies--

Q: May I interrupt, Sir. Wasn't that a kind of retrogression? It's the sort of thing you came away from, wasn't it?

Mr. K.: Well, we had organized after or during World War II very much on a basis that was to last about twenty-five years. We had persevered over this period, you might say, with the split between what goes on in a classroom and the management aspects of the schoolhouse, the instructional staffing and so on.

So, we were really changing from what had, in my opinion, been a pretty good concept, but we were being pushed into the position of looking for some different way to organize.

Q: But it was the kind of concept that you helped develop, wasn't it, as a result of World War II experience?

Mr. K.: Yes, right, although the original format of the BuPers organization had been one that had been set forth by Boos, Fry, Allen, and Hamilton in 1942. They had indicated that there should be five divisions--or five sections-- of what later became the training division after World War II. And one of those sections, just in passing, was one called Physical Training, which as a matter of interest was headed by Gene Tunney, who was then on active duty in the Navy and with whom I became friendly as a colleague. After the war, we scaled down into two divisions, one of which, in effect, put instructional materials and methods in one bundle, and management aspects across the hall, so to speak, in another bundle, and that was the way we carried on business for something on the order of twenty years after World War II.

Q: Did it make you the least bit unhappy that you were going to reorganize in this new form?

Mr. K.: Personally, I didn't have the same concern in the need for reorganization as some other people in the organization did. We were pressed at that time fairly consistently by a naval officer who had been taking a course at George Washington University, I think it was, in how to manage. He came up with ideas of how we ought to reorganize. What we really came up with eventually was not one that made him very happy, but at least we came up with a reorganization. And, as I've said, Admiral Freeman, having come from the Weapons Systems electronics arena, was convinced that this was the right way to go--to align ourselves with the Weapons Systems organizations that were coming into being throughout the Navy Department. I had no real concern about that particular aspect of it. I think perhaps that it was wise to try to make sure that we had comparability in our organization with the impending, forthcoming weapons systems arena.

Q: Besides, it makes for a more harmonious working arrangement, doesn't it?

Mr. K.: Right. But when the responsibility for creating this reorganization fell principally on me, why, I found myself with quite a problem to go in these two directions. One, to organize in such a way that you reflected weapons systems and made it stand out in the organization titles, but at the same time you put military personnel at the points of decision, which had not been the case before. At least, the organization chart didn't show it that way.

We had, for example, large sections which were headed by civilian professional educators. The new organization got away from that. We did have, as I've said, the four divisions and each of those was headed by a military man. We maintained, however, a degree of continuity by putting civilians further down into the organization but in a position to carry on over the years as the military changed.

Q: The traditional role of the Civil Service!

Mr. K.: Right. We also set up a fairly extensive staff. I've already mentioned the programming office, which became a vital element in the new organization and it was composed of a civilian staff. It had what amounted to veto power over the planning aspects, at least, as they came in from the various divisions. This was not veto in the sense of "you can't have that" but veto in the sense of "here is what we think ought to be the highest priorities and therefore, where you will give the most emphasis."

Another civilian group was called the Assistant for Instruction. This was also a relatively powerful group in the sense of talented professionals who exerted a considerable amount of influence on the methodology and particularly in the innovations field, for which we by that time had felt a need. In other words, things like computer-assisted instruction and so on were coming onto the horizon. It was necessary to keep up to date with these things and what was going on in the outside world, the civilian educational world, and so on. So a fairly extensive group of about six or eight professional civilians were in that organization. These latter two that I mentioned were staff offices, however, so we still had military in the decision points.

Q: Tell me about the care that was exercised in the appointment of the military to sit in at these points of decision.

Mr. K.: You took what you could get usually, like you do in most military assignments.

Q: But some are more qualified than others.

Mr. K.: Oh, yes. We were fortunate in being able to exert sufficient influence on the detailing of people to the Bureau of Naval Personnel to get some good talent and to be pretty choosey in the kinds of talent we got.

Q: This called for vigilance, though?

Mr. K.: It was an element of management that you continually watched over pretty carefully and tried to make sure that you got your share of the good people.

As I've said, this problem of distributing equitably the available civilian and military talent in terms of billets and bodies was one that caused us to face an organizational trauma that at times seemed to me to be infeasible. Its accomplishment stands out in my memory as the mecca of the many organizational changes which I have had a part in or have participated in considering.

I have previously noted that the Navy leaders in 1946 decided to retain two fleet training commands. Many efforts were made over the years to describe clearly the function of these commands, their relationship to the fleet and to BuPers. Essentially, the fleet training commanders were under the military command of the fleet commanders in chief, and certain shore activities reported to them. But BuPers provided funds, overhead staff billets, people, facilities, equipment, a large proportion of students, pedagogical advice and assistance. Most of the time the thing worked pretty well because people made it work. Obviously, there were problems at times, such as a sonar man trained on the West Coast did not have the same credentials as one trained on the East Coast.

And there was no authority to referee. In cases like this OpNav sometimes requested BuPers to serve as a referee.

We in BuPers finally wrote an instruction in the early 1960s, I think, issued, first, as a BuPers document and later as a CNO document, which described in some considerable detail the functions to be performed by fleet CinCs and their subordinates and those to be accomplished by BuPers for fleet schools ashore, such as sonar schools, amphibious training units, the submarine school, fleet training centers, etc.

This worked well until the Navy's concept of RMS threw things into a tailspin in 1967 by insisting that funds should flow along command lines. This created chaos in the sense that funds which previously flowed through BuPers now went through the fleet CinCs. They also formulated the military construction programs for fleet schools. However, BuPers still managed the military billets and assignment of people and purchased training devices. Thus, an activity got its money for civilian billets and facilities from one source, and military billets and bodies, part of its student loading and training devices, for which no facilities might have been provided, from another source.

Q: Did any notable conflicts arise as a result of this?

Mr. K.: Yes, we had many examples. Of course, it was obvious that a field activity got its civilian population, its civilian staffing, by one set of circumstances and its military by another, and nowhere was there anybody that could amalgamate those two things.

Q: Other than in Washington?

Mr. K.: Well, there wasn't anybody in Washington any more that could do that really, or that was in a position to do it, or had a mission to do it. We had instances where training devices were procured through the budgetary process, which, as you know, is a long-drawn-out affair. We found ourselves a couple of times with devices on hand, money to purchase them, but no building in which to put the devices because the building had fallen out since that was somebody else's responsibility. This resulted in a management dichotomy in which you no longer, in effect, had a viable referee.

BuPers highlighted this dichotomy to OpNav and this resulted in the Navy Inspector General being directed to study the matter. The Inspector General studied a long time and after one or two starts in other directions finally settled on a recommendation that Op-37--this was then the OpNav focal point for training be transferred from Op-03 to Op-01 (the deputy CNO for manpower), where it became Op-01C, and that fleet schools ashore operate under the military command of the Chief of Naval Personnel, but with fleet CinCs to retain a strong voice.

A complicating factor in all of this was the fact that fleet training ashore was a concern not only of the fleet training commanders, but certain other type commanders.

Submarine forces, amphibious forces, cruiser-destroyer forces, and mine forces were vitally interested in specialty schools. So the problem was complex. Its solution, however, was given some impetus by a study of the Navy's training organization being conducted concurrently by the GAO. In other words, the Navy was impelled to come up with some solution to this problem because it faced the GAO study with some trepidation and therefore this was a continuing pressure.

Q: How did the GAO come into it? Were the expenditures suspect?

Mr. K.: The normal operating procedure in the GAO, as I'm sure you're aware, is to look around and find out where they can put their fingers and see where they can discover a problem that they can survey into. I suspect that they had talked with somebody in the training organization and they had become aware that there was a dichotomy, as I described it. It's my recollection that this happened in Norfolk by actually talking with somebody in the field concerning how they were getting along, you might say. So the GAO instituted a fairly considerable study over a rather protracted period. Their representatives met with us in BuPers and they had their field people investigating the field organizations. It's not unusual for GAO to take an interest in this sort of thing. In fact, today we've got the GAO investigating many arenas in the training situation.

Q: Well, they constitute something of a watch dog, don't they?

Mr. K.: This is their purpose, as they see it. Anyway, they had begun a study of this thing.

To make a long story short, we arranged for the CNO to sponsor a Fleet-OpNav-BuPers conference in Washington in June 1970. At that time BuPers and fleet reps reached agreement in a statement of functional responsibilities. This statement which, in slightly modified form to reflect the recent reorganization of the training establishment, is still extant. It placed the fleet schools and the training commanders under the command of the Chief of Naval Personnel, but preserved specified functions as responsibilities of the fleet CinCs and their type commanders. The initial agreement was issued as an OpNav instruction signed by Admiral Bernard A. "Chick" Clarey, who was then VCNO.

This had the effect of making dollars, military and civilian dollars, military people, facilities, equipment and other support all flow in the same channel. It restored BuPers to a position where a substantial degree of coordination and integration could be exercised.

The GAO report, which came out soon after this event, noted this action as being apparently in their opinion a satisfactory solution.

Q: Had their findings been anticipated in the development

of this new directive?

Mr. K.: In reality, the GAO report said, well, we've looked into this, watched the Navy come to the conclusion that this is the way they ought to go, and, as far as we can see, this is the right way to go. However, we would suggest to the Secretary of the Navy that he keep an eye on progress, as the plan develops into the future.

This was the end, up to this date, anyway, of the GAO's concern and interest in the training organization as a total organization.

Q: Was the CNO himself interested in this conference? Did he involve himself?

Mr. K.: The VCNO, Admiral Clarey, got very concerned and we had several sessions with him. He was an old friend of ours in BuPers whom we'd known back in the days when he was in the submarine business. He took a personal interest and did appear for a rather extensive period at the conference with the BuPers, CNO, and fleet reps that I referred to before. He took a vital interest in it. Of course, he was in somewhat of a spot because he was in a position where he was about to tell the fleet commanders in chief, who were pretty vitally interested personally and very high level, that this was the way we were going to operate. In other words, that certain of their shore establishments were going to be removed from their command.

There was a lot of apprehension, on the part of senior people in the fleet commands and particularly on the part of the type commanders, especially ComSubLant and, to a lesser degree, ComSubPac--concern that they were going to lose some kind of control that they thought they needed.

Q: I suppose particularly because of Polaris programs?

Mr. K.: Well, they were really more vitally interested in the whole panorama. Of course, the fleet submarine training facility at Pearl Harbor was very close to SubPac's interest. The submarine school in New London has always been very vital to SubLant. So they were concerned that somebody was going to put a finger in the pie and that they were going to lose some degree of control.

So it was a rather tenuous kind of a situation and it affected real high level people in the Navy. I think we were real fortunate to come out as well as we did.

Q: Tell me about your personal role in this development.

Mr. K.: My personal role in it was rather considerable. We got together the presentations that we gave to the Inspector General and met with his people almost continuously for months in trying to be of help in shaping his position and the direction that he was going. Then later, after he had made his recommendations, we briefed Admiral Clarey as to what way we wanted to go--we thought was best to go. This resulted in several sessions with Admiral Clarey, discussions which included the Op-03 people. You recall that Op-37 was a part of Op-03 at that time and he was the OpNav focal point for training so-called. Therefore, he had a decided interest in it. Op-01 was in the picture, and so there were many interested parties.

We went through all of this in the spring of 1970, and finally got Admiral Clarey to decide, after a considerable amount of correspondence back and forth between him to agree that the way we should proceed was to have a conference in Washington. This conference was to determine not that we were going to do it but how we were going to do this matter of bringing the fleet schools ashore under the command of the Chief of Naval Personnel.

Q: Taking for granted that it's going to be done?

Mr. K.: This is what we're going to do but we're going to protect the interests of the fleets, therefore you fellows send your boys in and we'll all get together and wrestle this thing out.

At the meeting, which was on the 4th of June 1970, we all sat around the table and reached what you might consider the basic conclusions.

Q: Was this easy to accomplish or was it difficult?

Mr. K.: There was a good deal of conversation, in which the fleet commanders represented by their training commanders were anxious to make sure that their interests were covered. There was a good deal of conversation about who was going to finance these activities ashore. In other words, who would have control over the finances. You can see that this was a vital interest because he who has the money has the control.

Q: An old adage!

Mr. K.: Right. This was one of the concerns that the fleet expressed a great deal of interest in. But we were able to hold our position pretty solidly and came out with what we went in looking for insofar as the major considerations were concerned. Having reached this point, having reported to Admiral Clarey, we met with a group from the fleet to thrash out the next day the words to put down on paper. That became the instruction that Admiral Clarey signed.

You asked what part did I play. Well, one of the things I did was to chair the meeting to put the words on paper and to issue this paper. It really wasn't as difficult as it may sound because we had gone through this several times in the 1960s. We were pretty sure of our ground. We knew what the functions were that the fleet wanted--what we were willing to let them have, you might say. We knew also what functions of management had to be kept in the hands of the Chief of Naval Personnel so that we could play a vital role in refereeing not only the matter of what kind of training went on in the fleet schools but also how did it fit into and integrate with the training that was going to be conducted in other schools under the management of the Chief of Naval Personnel.

Q: As you recount this, I see a series of concentric circles. I mean the personnel situation seemed to go round in circles through the years. Is that a true observation?

Mr. K.: Yes, I think it's very true. We speak of it in terms of training programs, the emphasis, and the organization itself, going in cycles. We had pretty much of a sine curve effect in which, at one time on the way up, you were getting pressure from one direction, then you'd get a lessening of that pressure. This is perhaps fortunate in a way because you're then in a position to look back and see what you did when this same thing came up a few years before.

Q: It makes you somewhat philosophical, doesn't it?

Mr. K.: Yes. I think this is a truism also. As I've gotten older I've come to have that philosophy. In fact, we're facing a rather traumatic situation at the minute. I find myself counseling the younger folks in the organization who tend to look upon this as the greatest emergency that has faced the Navy in all of history by saying, in effect, don't worry about it too much because we've gone through this kind of thing before. While we can't see our way out of the dilemma right now, we've managed to work ouselves out, over the past thirty years, of several of these kinds of critical times.

Q: As an aftermath to this new arrangement in 1970, did you get any repercussions from fleet commanders?

Mr. K.: We had only outstanding success in our relationships with the fleet commanders, with the training commanders and with the fleet training activities. It really restored us to, you might say, a position we had been in for many years and therefore continued in the same vein what we had enjoyed in the past.

Q: Admiral Clarey himself, as a fleet commander, is he entirely happy with what he promulgated?

Mr. K.: I have seen no evidence to the contrary on the part of either CinCLantFleet or CinCPacFleet so far as the operation has gone on. Of course, the training commanders and the type commanders are still there. To come up to date to a degree, the fleet training commanders are now under the commander of the Chief of Naval Training. That is, ComTraLant and ComTraPac, operate under the command of the Chief of Naval Training and this, in effect, carries on very much in the same fashion the responsibility that they had for fleet schools, and that part of the training organization for which they have responsibility, as was the case when they reported to the Chief of Naval Personnel before.

There has been an effort on the part of the Chief of

Naval Training--not a new effort really, but emphasis on it--to make sure that the fleet training commanders are brought into the fold continuously. So at conferences, such as was held recently in Pensacola, the fleet training commanders from each of the two coasts were among the subordinate commanders participating. I think the new command is fortunately much better fortified in the numbers of its flag officers in comparison with the number of flag officers that were available and took part in the organization when the Bureau of Naval Personnel was carrying on or conducting 70 to 80 percent of the training.

This, you might say, is one of the advantages because you've got much more horsepower in the field than we used to have.

This brings us to a point where we can consider briefly the most recent and most awesome effort to reorganize training.

Q: The Cagle Board?

THE CAGLE BOARD REORGANIZATION

Mr. K.: Yes. A reorganization that this time was accomplished.

We had noted the continuing high-level concern for Navy education and training organization over the years since World War II, when it was essentially concentrated in the Bureau of Naval Personnel. First came the separation of air training from BuPers early in World War II and then periodically examination through the Hopwood, Pride, Freeman, Dillon, INSGEN, and GAO studies in an effort to find a means of doing the education-training job better and more efficiently. It will be recalled that the situation was examined rather thoroughly by the CNO's Training Policy Board right after World War II. The decision then was to maintain the status quo. That is, air training under Op-05 with an extensive Chief of Naval Air Training (CNATRA) Field command; medical under BuMed; afloat training under Op-03 and the fleet CinCs; and all the other either under or supported by BuPers. The net result of all the boards was to continue to maintain the status quo, except that surface and subsurface reserve training came to have a functional commander who was, however, still supported by BuPers, and the formation of Op-03T, later Op-37, and still later Op-01C, as the training focal point in OpNav.

Q: Sir, the fact that these various boards decided to maintain the status quo, does this underscore the fact that the system was the correct one?

Mr. K.: Well, I think it was under the circumstances, but there are some who say unkindly that BuPers succeeded in maintaining the status quo in the period from World War II until 1971 when the Cagle Board was formed. The basic theme employed by BuPers over these years in resisting change was that education-training is something that happens to people and therefore is an integral part of personnel management. Accordingly, it was contended that if a change was to be made it should be toward bringing the air training and Reserve training into the people management arena and placing all shore-based training under the Chief of Naval Personnel.

However, the charter of the Cagle Board was different than that assigned to the previous study groups. The others had been charged with examining the organization and recommending changes therein. The Cagle Board was told, in effect, to assume that there would be a single training command and its charter was, then, to devise and implement plans for making it so.

Q: And it was told by whom?

Mr. K.: By, ostensibly, the Chief of Naval Operations, although the actual directive--the charter of the Cagle Board--was signed by the Chief of Naval Personnel. The following excerpt from the charter is significant:

> "For the purpose of developing an implementation plan for a single naval training command in the field."

Other significant phrases included:

> "Specifically, the plan should provide for the removal from Washington of the majority of the organization of the Assistant Chief of Naval Personnel for Education and Training per se."

This, of course, stated firmly that responsibility for education and training would be removed from the

Bureau of Naval Personnel.

In addition to the formation of a single field training program, the precept of the Cagle Board directed that the board examine a tightened organization within OpNav to establish policy, determine training objectives and priorities, to support the manpower, equipment, facilities, and funding resources for the training establishment. It may be of interest to note that the precept for the Cagle Board was written within Pers C in BuPers and signed by the then chief of Naval Personnel, Vice Admiral D. H. Guinn, with, I am sure, the concurrence and support of the Chief of Naval Operations.

Board membership consisted, in addition to the chairman, Rear Admiral Malcolm W. Cagle, of naval officer representatives of BuPers; Deputy CNO for Manpower; Assistant Deputy CNO for Reserve Manpower; Deputy CNO for Aviation; Chief of Naval Air Technical Training; BuMed; Chief of Naval Air Training; CinCLant Fleet; CinCPacFleet; Deputy CNO for Fleet Readiness; Director, Navy Program Planning, Office of CNO: and the U. S. Marine Corps. There were no civilian members of the board.

Q: How did this come about, and how was Admiral Cagle selected to be the chairman of the board?

Mr. K.: I'm not sure that I can answer that question. Personally, Admiral Cagle has told me that he was called in by Admiral Zumwalt and told that he was to head up this board. He was at that time holding an office in Op-05 in the Chief of Naval Operations office. He has indicated that he was reluctant to undertake it but he looked upon it as an order and therefore marched off.

Q: Did he have any particular background in this area?

Mr. K.: Admiral Cagle has had many varied and extremely important assignments in the Navy, but I don't recall any specifically that would, you might say, earmark him or tag him as being particularly interested in or concerned with training as a function. However, an aviation officer is vitally interested in the training of pilots and, being a member of the staff of Op-5, this was one of the resources to which the aviation organization would look forward.

I'm quite sure that it had been determined, but I'm not sure by whom, that the board would be headed up by an aviation officer, that is a 1300 officer, and that Admiral Cagle either was more available or considered by some to be more qualified and available than perhaps some other 1300 officers might have been at the time.

Q: Why was it determined that it would be an all-military board?

Mr. K.: I have no good answer for that either. I have often speculated on--I'll not answer that question directly for the minute--but I've often speculated on the reason for the apparently arbitrary CNO decision to remove education and training from BuPers and thus separate the training people function from other people-management functions, such as recruiting, procurement, job assignment, welfare, and other aspects of career development. Many others have speculated also. Some say it's understood that the CNO, Admiral Zumwalt, was disenchanted with the BuPers education-training operation during his previous duty tour in BuPers some seventeen years prior to the formation of the Cagle Board. Others say he was under pressure to move people out of Washington and the training organization lent itself readily to this objective.

It's my impression, however, that in connection with a reorganization of BuPers, the Chief of Naval Personnel recommended to the CNO the amalgamation of surface/sub-surface training with air training, and the CNO saw no good reason to say no. It is significant to note that the Chief of Naval Personnel at that time was the first and only, up to this time, 1300 category officer to serve as the Chief of Naval Personnel.

Q: Who was he?

Mr. K.: Admiral Guinn. So, in further answer to your question about why was it an all-military board, I can only hark back to the premise that was voiced by Admiral Fitzhugh Lee some years previous that civilian influence in BuPers was too vigorous. Perhaps Admiral Guinn, who had a large part in the formation of the board and the membership thereof, held an opinion somewhat similar to Admiral Fitzhugh Lee's and therefore saw to it that it was an all-military board.

Q: I think you said sometime past that Admiral Lee had a reformation in his thinking afterwards.

Mr. K.: Yes, I said that later on in his career Admiral Lee and I got to be on more friendly terms and I think I succeeded in convincing him that the situation in BuPers was not as bad as he had previously considered that it was. I can't relate, however, unfortunately, that I ever succeeded in reaching that point as far as Admiral Guinn was concerned!

Q: You have with Admiral Cagle!

Mr. K.: I'm not sure of that really, frankly, to lay the cards on the table. Admiral Cagle has always been kind and thoughtful in his personal attention to and his attitude toward me. However, I think that there has been in the new organization a diminution of the influence of civilians in their relationships to the vital areas, let's say. There's no doubt in my mind that, as we did in BuPers, there has been a trend in the direction of making sure that the military occupy the decision points in the new organization. I'm not against that, but I'm convinced that there are a number of talented and qualified, highly qualified, civilian educators whose talents are not being looked upon as being vital in connection with the operations of the training command. This situation has undoubtedly prompted the earlier retirement, or relocation of other highly talented education/training managers.

This is, perhaps you might say, a continuation of the previous position that has been taken within the Air organization of the Navy, the air training organization. They have considered over the years that they could look to civilians for research or pedagogical advice, but when it came to management functions there was always a tendency-- a strong influence--by the military to assure that civilians did not occupy strong management positions.

Such speculation is now, of course, an item of curiosity only.

Q: Interested curiosity!

Mr. K.: The Cagle Board was formed and labored mightily from February till June 1971. The team visited more than sixty commands and activities, consulted more than one hundred experts, including at least one member of the Pride Board and two former naval Inspectors General and three former Assistant Chiefs of Naval Personnel for education and training. I might say, at this point, that Admiral Fitzhugh Lee was one of the individuals who was consulted by Admiral Cagle.

It was a comprehensive effort. The Chairman and the various panels of the board invited me liberally into their discussions. I, of course, had sense enough not to fight any longer for the status quo since the die was cast and the problem that remained was the selection of an organization. To this end I offered my advice freely and without reservation. In retrospect, I am unable to recall any areas in which my advice succeeded in influencing materially the board's decisions. Accordingly, I am in the happy position of being able to observe objectively, with no intention of claiming credit for any successes of the new organization or accepting responsibility for any of its failures, if it has any.

Q: That's quite a good position to be in!

Mr. K.: The Cagle Board was emphatic in its position that all Navy training--all Navy education and training--except BuMed be commanded by one officer. BuMed training being small and highly specialized would be allowed to operate as in the past.

Q: Would you give me some of that past background, Sir?

Mr. K.: In my knowledge of the situation, BuMed has always been specified in <u>Navy Regulations</u> as being in charge of medical training in the Navy. The latest extant edition of <u>Navy Regs</u> indicates that, in effect, there are two Navy training agencies in the Navy, one of those being the Chief of the Bureau of Medicine and Surgery and the other being the Chief of the Bureau of Naval Personnel. With respect to the latter there is a clause which says the Bureau of Naval Personnel is responsible for all training and education, except that which is assigned to other authorities. Up to this point, however, I have no knowledge--or at least up until the reorganization effected by the Cagle Board, no other document existed which assigned the responsibility for education and training to any other agencies.

Q: Did the Chaplains' Corps enjoy the same sort of a special status?

Mr. K.: No. None of the other corps, to include the Chaplains' Corps or the Supply Corps, the Civil Engineer Corps, or any of the other staff officers of the Navy, ever had responsibility assigned directly to them to support or manage their own training. These have always been in my memory responsibilities of the Chief of Naval Personnel, at least in recent years. So it's been only BuMed that's outside by itself.

I suspect that in the early days this came about because of the importance given then as now to the healing arts as being something which really nobody quarrels with and it's allowed to be its own fraternity, so to speak. It probably came about as a result of political aspirations on the part of the Medical Corps back in the days when the Navy was reaching its earlier history.

Accordingly, the Cagle Board, considering the fact that BuMed training was small and highly specialized and has always been operated separately in the past, recommended that it should be left in status quo. However, provision was made for coordination by having an additional duty representative of the Bureau of Medicine and Surgery on the staff of the Director, Naval Education and Training in OpNav. This has been done.

Q: This is for cognizance purposes?

Mr. K.: Cognizance and coordination and liaison. In effect, OpNav Op-099 does exert a degree of influence over the Bureau of Medicine and Surgery. For example, we have been recently engaged in considering with the other services, the Army, Air Force, and Marine Corps, additional inter-service training. As a part of this exercise, we have brought in the BuMed representative to sit with his counterparts from the other services. So, in effect, the training organization, (Op-099, and the Chief of Naval Training), is positively causing the Bureau of Medicine and Surgery to come into the fold.

Q: Up to the present time, has anyone within Personnel been charged with taking a gander at the effectiveness of their system of training?

Mr. K.: No, not to my knowledge, although actually the Bureau of Naval Personnel sets forth the requirements for medical and dental personnel in the same manner that it sets forth the requirements for the ratings, like machinists' mates or electronics technicians throughout the rest of the Navy. So there is that influence.

Insofar as any relationship to what goes on in the schoolhouse, the CNT/OpNav organization has not assumed any responsibility with respect to medical training. I'm sure that the Inspector General, for example, looks in on their activities the same as he does other activities. I'm sure also that medical training is not immune from attack by the GAO if the GAO were inclined to attack! But, principally, the Bureau of Medicine and Surgery operates by itself.

Thus, all the air, surface, subsurface, regular and reserve education and training would be coagulated under one directorate, as the Cagle Board prescribed. Provision was made for the strong focal point in OpNav by the formation of the Director of Naval Education and Training, (DNET), to monitor all training, make Navy-wide training policy, set priorities, and program for and defend training resources.

In addition to DNET, the Cagle Board elected to establish training divisions in the offices of the Deputy CNO for Submarines and the Deputy for Surface Warfare. In effect, these officers were designed to emulate the similar air training office, which had been in existence in the office of the Deputy CNO for Air and which was credited as the key factor in the recognized success of naval air training.

The Cagle Board's initial recommendations were altered in two respects.

Q: When did they submit those recommendations?

Mr. K.: In June of 1971 and they were approved in time for the formation of the Chief of Naval Training by the 1st of August 1971.

The two respects that were altered were: 1) management of education, meaning essentially the U. S. Naval Academy, the Naval War College, the PG School, and NROTC programs, was retained in Washington under the command of CNO (DNET), and 2) the Reserve training both air, which had been a part of CNATRA previously, and surface were segregated from regular Navy sub-surface/surface/air flight training.

The situation regarding education was eased some by the fact that Vice Admiral Cagle was double-hatted as DNET and the Chief of Naval Training. However, in reality, the power resides in Pensacola, since the Admiral is present there more often than in Washington and since he willed it that way.

Q: You're there a great deal also, aren't you?

Mr. K.: We have a lot of travel back and forth with people from Pensacola being here and people from here being in Pensacola. Most of the command meetings such as the meeting of the subordinate commanders, which I seem to remember was held last in October, are held in Pensacola. So when meetings such as that are convened, people from here journey to Pensacola. So we have under the present circumstances people on their way to Pensacola or from Pensacola here in a steady stream. Admiral Cagle has arranged for a fleet of airplanes which we, in BuPers, were never fortunate in having in the older days. He uses them to get people back and forth and to journey around the command in much better and faster fashion than we were able to do in the old days.

Q: How did you travel in those days?

Mr. K.: Well, you went, but you didn't go very often. You went singly and you didn't engage in as many conferences where you got large groups of people representing various components of the command together, because you just didn't have the Navy air capability for collecting people together in the fashion that now is feasible. There are planes which run constantly between here and Pensacola. He has--I'm not sure how many--but two or three T-39s, for example, which are small jets which will carry up to four passengers, and you can make the trip from here to Pensacola in about two flying hours. Larger planes are available, like one or more C-131s, which will carry many more passengers but don't go as fast and therefore it's a long time in the air.

The Chief of Naval Training was made the major claimant (financial manager) for education and training programs, even though the command for education resided in the office of the Chief of Naval Operations. It was evident from the start that this would produce difficulties because resources flowed through Pensacloa. That staff was not equipped to make program management decisions for education programs. On the other hand, DNET had the program knowledge but could not regulate the flow of resources to education programs. This situation will be improved when, as has now been approved, responsibility for education programs transits to Pensacola in March 1973. This will place education where the Cagle Board originally recommended. Countrarywise, Reserve training seems destined to remain outside the CNT fold, for political reasons.

Q: What would they be?

Mr. K.: Well, there is great concern, for example, in the Congress for Reserve training. This is one of those grass-roots kinds of things. The Reserves are people that are in the home locations and therefore have a considerable influence on their congressmen, and Congress is very anxious to make sure that Reserve training gets proper support. It has set up safeguards to assure it, such as setting aside special budget machinery to protect and assure that the Reserves get what the Reserves think they need and the Congress agrees that they need.

Special offices have been established in the office of the Secretary of Defense to guard the Reserve prestige, and this filters down into the Navy which is prevailed upon to assure that the Reserves get the proper attention.

So what has been done, after a large number of studies--a series of studies--on what to do with Reserve training, is that Reserve training for other-than-air and Reserve training for air are now going to be amalgamated under a single command, whose headquarters will be in New Orleans. Thus, we get a joining up of Reserve training, but the entire Reserve training establishment remains isolated or separate from the training organization for the regular Navy.

Q: In your opinion, is this a real loss?

Mr. K.: In my opinion the Reserves would fare just as well, if not better, if they were actually organized in such a way that the one who was in charge of regular Navy training was charged with the responsibility for the training of Reserves.

Q: Would this save in expenditures?

Mr. K.: I'm not sure that there would be any great saving. I think that it might reduce the overhead perhaps, the number of commands that are required. But, essentially, the Reserve is what you might consider a locally oriented organization. People are near home towns. However, when it comes to receiving modern, updated training, they usually are beholden to the regular Navy to get on a regular Navy ship for training or to get into a regular Navy school, since the Reserves can't operate schools that duplicate those of the Navy. Therefore, the problems of integration of Reserve training and assuring that Reserves are kept up to date in their training would be eased if you had the responsibility resting in one organization.

Q: Has this argument been made from time to time to the Congress?

Mr. K.: I'm not sure that there's ever been an opportunity to get it to the Congress or to make that kind of a position to the Congress. It is historical fact that the Reserves, the Reserve organization, Reserve demands, have always fared better through the Congress than has the regular Navy for its requirements. So from a purely Reserve point of view, I'm sure that the Reserves feel they're profiting by being watched after by the Congress, and if this special brand of watching requires for them to be organized separately, why, then, this is good. I have no doubt but that the Reserve Officers Association, which over the years has had as its leaders some former active duty officers, has had a considerable influence and continues to have considerable influence in guiding the Congress.

Q: Mr. Kenyon, I don't know whether this is the appropriate time to introduce this and ask you for comment, or whether you would prefer to do it another time. I recall Fitzhugh Lee talking at some length and with some firm convictions on the subject, he was contrasting the educational standards in the world at large, the public schools, with the training offered in the Navy and he saw a great difference. He felt the standards in the Navy were so much higher and he lamented the fact that nothing could be done about the other sector.

Mr. K.: I would agree that the standards are real high within the Navy. They are looked at by many different people, not only the management within the Navy itself, but also as I've previously indicated, by people like the Inspector General and auditors of various kinds who are always looking for ways in which you can reduce your overhead and do things cheaper. But there is a purpose, I think, in Navy education and training which may not be so readily apparent in civilian education in the usual sense. You have the capability of establishing targets, the production that you would like to get out of your training program and your organization. Therefore, you have a better means of orienting your training effort in the direction of the target that you have set for yourself. Contrary-wise, in civilian education institutions, including colleges and secondary schools and various other kinds of schools, education is an amorphous thing that most anybody could make a judgment on as to what is that you want to accomplish.

There are people who think that what you want to accomplish is that an individual can be able to figure out what his grocery bill is. This, perhaps, can be identified as one of the real objectives of education in civilian schools, but, in general, a clear definion of target is lacking. Accordingly, what do you judge civilian education against? I think you can judge it better in the Navy because you've got some target that you were shooting for and you can say we reached the target or we didn't reach the target.

On the other hand, I think that it would be inappropriate to point the finger in generalities against all civilian education as it exists because I'm sure that there's a lot of it that is really worthwhile and really well done. I can speak with some assurance on this because I came into my Navy working experience through the school teacher route. I know, therefore, from that experience and my later experience in teaching in night school at George Washington University that there are a lot of real highly qualified educators in the education business. I can further support the argument by indicating that the majority of the educators that we have had in our Navy educational and training circles came into the Navy, lots of them in the World War II period. Therefore a good deal of the success of the Navy program, I think, can be attributed to the civilian educators that we took out of the civilian academic world.

So, while I would agree that there's no doubt but that Navy education and training is well done and well targeted, I wouldn't want to make any unfair criticisms of the civilian educational system.

Q: I think Admiral Lee was wrestling with something more immediate in terms of the material coming to him for training from private life and having to be--having to have what they knew fortified by what the Navy could give them.

Mr. K.: I can illustrate the distinction, perhaps, that he may have had in mind. We have made experimentation in the past and we still have some going on today whereby we have contracted with civilian schools to carry on certain training. We have one going at the minute, for example, in two different activities. We have contracted with them to train our prospective electronics technicians. We have pretty much decreed what the subject matter will be and the courses which are taught by those institutions, but we are finding that it takes a longer period to get over the same ground in a civilian school than we afford for that same material in the Navy. We also find that it is necessary for the Navy to add on some specifics, particularly with respect to Navy equipment which the ET schools, so to speak, in the civilian world don't have. So, from the Navy's point of view, we think at this stage of the game, although the pilot programs haven't been completed, that we can teach people what the Navy needs to have the individual know in a shorter term and cover more ground than we can buy on the outside.

This is not to say, though, that that institution, for the purpose for which it was established and for the students that it turns out for civilian life, is not doing a real bang-up job.

Q: In terms of Navy objectives, would you say that discipline is an element involved in this?

Mr. K.: I don't believe that is a strong element. Of course, the Navy school would have a tendency toward discipline, but I think that in a trade school in civilian life that--I'm speaking now of a private school where the individual is paying his tuition and therefore is anxious to get his money's worth out of his effort--you really wouldn't find a lot of difference in discipline in that kind of school. In public schools discipline, I'm sure, is a problem these days. However, there are many schools where I think that the personality of the individual administrators and teachers has succeeded in keeping discipline a minimal problem.

Q: Thank you for that digression.

Mr. K.: We were talking about the segregation of Naval Reserve training away from regular Navy training. The way things have come out it appears that one of the principal purposes of the Cagle Board effort--to get all Navy education and training consolidated--seems to have missed the target, at least for the time being.

Q: What is the prognosis on that?

Mr. K.: It would be my guess that the new Reserve training command is going to exist for a long number of years to come. It brings into sight a need for a lot of coordination and collaboration, in my mind, between the Chief of Naval Reserve Training and the Chief of Naval Training. I'm sure that this can and will be accomplished, however, as time goes along.

In any case, even without Reserve training, the education and training organization is big and its problems challenging. It's not my role or my purpose to judge the merits of the new education and training enterprise. It has my sympathy and my assistance to the extent I'm qualified and able to give it. Only time will tell its effective ness or lack of it. Suffice it to say that Vice Admiral Cagle, who is a dynamic hard-working leader, deserves the support of all hands in what seems often, to me and maybe sometimes to him, a stupendous perhaps impossible task in an era of unreasonable curtailment. He has collected a talented staff, especially in Pensacola, who likewise are working hard, grappling with serious problems of far reaching scope and significance.

A number of courageous management curtailment actions have been taken already and others are in the offing. I will make one more point regarding the new organization before leaving it and going back to the safer, more historical ground. The BuPers education and training organization was a centrally directed and managed enterprise, operated, controlled directly from Washington. This was different than the system used by the Army, Air Force, or the Naval Air. As Admiral Strean, who was then CNATRA, expressed it to me, the naval air training organization was a "loosely decentralized" one. There seems to be evidence now in sight that Admiral Cagle is leaning toward a type of centralized organization. Again, only time will tell.

Q: Do you want to comment, Sir, at this point on the increased cost of naval education? You mentioned Admiral Strean and I remember what he said to us back in 1970 about the tremendous expense of educating a naval pilot, for instance, the increase was a fabulous one.

Mr. K.: Like everything else, there has been a continual increase in the cost of training on the whole, and in the cost of training an individual, whether he's a pilot or an electronics technician or what. Much of this increase in cost has been due to the inflationary aspects which we all have contended with in recent years. Salaries have been going up rapidly, both in the civilian world and in the military world, and accordingly the cost of training has been rising real rapidly. However, this has not been out of proportion with the rise in other areas of the civilian economy or other areas within the military.

Q: Do you see any crippling effects to the program as a result of the obvious budgetary cuts that we're facing now?

Mr. K.: Yes, there will be crippling effects that bring real serious management problems because what you're really wrestling with now is a matter of priorities. Where shall I put my resources so as to take care of the Number One requirement and the Number Two requirement and let some of the other areas which we have been supporting in the past be of secondary concern? Therefore, you face a difficult problem right now in this connection. It is true, I'm sure, that because of the reorganization and the unsettling effect of the transition to a new organization these problems have become greater than they might otherwise have been. However, I would note that we have in the past gone through the Louis Johnson austerity era and we have gone through various other difficult times when training was being reduced. There's always a sentiment in the Navy against training. Navy training represents in terms of military manpower something more than 20 percent of the total strength of the Navy and, accordingly, it is visible and large target at which the budget cutters take great delight in aiming darts. This has gone on over the years and we have weathered through so far and I'm sure we're going to weather through the present crisis.

Q: Is it possible to make a definitive list of priorities in the face of these cuts?

Mr. K.: Yes, I think it is. It's a difficult problem and it's one that we're wrestling with right now. The Chief of Naval Operations has sent out an instruction, for example, which tries to advise the operators in the field, and I don't mean the training field alone, how you decide which priority you put at the top of the list. This is primarily hardware-oriented and obviously it comes out that you put such things as the Polaris and the Poseidon and the guided missiles and so on pretty high on the list, and some other things are going to be lower on the list.

This particular process doesn't work very well, when you come to some other arenas like where do you put the Naval Academy and the postgraduate school, for example, in contention with Poseidon? So, it's a problem for which we don't have a computer model that will solve the problem for the Navy. It has to be resolved through a series of decisions at various levels, and one of those levels is the training organization itself. The training organization has to make a stab, you might say, at what you're going to put highest on the list. Somebody up the line along the way, I guess the Chief of Naval Operations or perhaps the Secretary of the Navy may overrule your decision as to what heads the priority list.

I recall in this connection fairly recently drawing up a priority listing in the sense of setting down what I considered at that time to be the fenced areas--those things that were high enough on the priority so that nobody would really want to throw any daggers at them. It was a fairly extensive list and Admiral Cagle said to me, "Where did that come from? Who made up that priority list?" I said, "I didn't know anywhere else to get one, so I made it up. But here's your chance, Admiral Cagle, if you don't like this list, you can make one of your own," which he didn't do at that time. But I'm illustrating how this thing has to be done. It's a matter of sitting down, not necessarily at any one time, and saying these are the high-priority areas and therefore, we're not going to touch those, but here are some other things.

A few months ago, however, to illustrate further, all of the commands in the Navy, including the fleet commanders and training command, were required by high authority to come up with a priority listing of all of the functions and activities which each of those commands supported. So the Chief of Naval Training called in what experts could be found immediately available and came up with such a list, which goes, in inverse order, from those things which we were about to disestablish and, therefore, we had a high priority for getting rid of, down to those which you might say were the untouchables. There is a specific list in existence which says this is the way we will tackle these things. Obviously, such a list doesn't endure forever. It's subject to change every time you've got new circumstances.

Q: Tell me at this point how you're doing it at Pensacola.

Mr. K.: Well, the military construction program is an example of the creation of a priority list. Each activity and each command, of course, has military construction projects that it would like to get into the congressional program. Therefore, each year it submits its list to headquarters and then various commands are invited to send representatives to Pensacola, at which point an over-all priority list for the entire training command is created. This is then sent up, through channels, and hopefully remains relatively intact so that you get to Congress with your priority listing. Obviously, you never get all that you would like to have and it becomes necessary, therefore, to order your activities and your items in priority in such a way that you get those things which are considered by human judgment to be the most vital for the organization as a whole.

Q: Do you want to turn your attention to some of the problems involved in this whole area?

SOME PROBLEM AREAS

Mr. K.: All right, Sir. Running through what I have said previously is the theme that technological change is one of the major hurdles for the service training program. In my period of association we have gone from the infancy of vacuum-tube radar and sonar and propeller planes, through nuclear power and weapons, to satellites, space explorations, and jet supersonic aircraft.

Q: Quite a span!

Mr. K.: Every one of these technological breakthroughs required a comparable instructional breakthrough. Otherwise, the gadget didn't work, as some of them didn't, such as the missile that didn't fire when President John F. Kennedy watched a programmed demonstration aboard ship shortly before the Cuban crisis.

When weapons didn't work or when fires occurred aboard ship, or where, as in the current era, 1,200-pound steam plants give trouble at sea, training catches it. The struggle to keep training in pace is tremendous when weapons development proceeds so rapidly. A partial quote from Admiral Page Smith writing the CNO and others when he was CinCLantFleet may express this difficulty better than I can:

> "Last and perhaps most important is the personnel problem. One of our shortcomings here appears to be inadequate accounting for personal requirements for manning new systems to be developed. I am convinced we must consider personnel as a prime ingredient of new fleet weapon systems. We must

not continue to overcommit personnel resources. Our present position is sufficiently critical. I do not put any of the blame for the low level of manning and the low level of experience on BuPers or the training establishment. Given the fact that about 50 percent of all recruits are trainable and we train them all in critical skills, given further the low attention rate in critical skills, there is little more to demand of sailors. I consider that our training establishment now accomplishes miracles. What I fear is that we are reaching a point where we cannot man our ships with adequate technical rates. Our ships are being sophisticated to the point where they're almost beyond our scope. Each new equipment demands at least double the number of ratings as its predecessor required. Recently I came across an excellent statement by Jimmy James, our recent BuShips Chief. He said, 'The ultra sophistication of our systems will soon defeat our operational forces.' I am just about convinced that that time has arrived."

Q: Man in a sense is outmoded by the technological advances?

Mr. K.: Well, yes, I think what he was saying is that we have rushed from one new development, or a new model of an old piece of equipment, to the point where the people/ training establishment was just not able to keep up with the research, the development, and the production of weapons and weapons systems.

Q: Doesn't he say more than that about the personnel, the incapability of absorbing?

Mr. K.: Well, I think perhaps he may have been implying that, but I would judge more that his point was that we ought to slow down some and let people have a chance to catch up, so to speak. People were capable but you had to take their capability into consideration when you developed hardware and give the people a chance to learn about that kind of hardware before you rush off into another kind of totally different hardware.

Q: But at the same time you're in competition with another system elsewhere in the world doing pretty much the same thing?

Mr. K.: That's right. There's a matter of management that enters into all of this. Again, it's one of placing the proper priority in the proper perspective so that people don't get lost and left behind. The training establishment faced these problems in a constant atmosphere of austerity, of course. Engaging as it does, as I said before, more than 20 percent of total Navy strength, it afforded a highly visible target for manpower and budget cutters, and they did cut. So the training establishment often found itself on its uppers. It was only by good management by training leaders in taking advantage of the upswings in the critical times of the Lebanon, Korean, and Vietnamese crises that gave the training establishment sufficient momentum to remain viable and effective.

I think perhaps at this point it's interesting to note that Navy planning and programming has, because there wasn't any better way of doing it probably, been based on what you might consider the linear planning system. This meant that if the Navy came down in the number of ships and the forces, then you looked to training and said, well, we'll cut the Navy training establishment proportionately with the decrease in the structure of the Navy. And these were the difficult times. The Navy training couldn't afford to be cut in proportion to the decrease from whatever level it had managed to acquire at that time, because activities like the Naval Academy, for example, are not functions linear with the strength of the Navy. Accordingly, when the Navy decreases in size and the linear application comes into being, the Navy training establishment suffers disproportionately.

On the other hand, when the Navy increases in size, as it did for the Lebanon and Korean and the Vietnamese crises and various other events like the Cuban crisis, then the linear effect gives an advantage to Navy training because it rises on a straight line with the rise in size of the Navy. Actually, the Navy training establishment is not then in need of that much of a rise in resources in order to take the new situation in stride.

Q: This is aimed toward the future?

Mr. K.: Because it is training for the future continually, anyway. Therefore, a relatively small rise in the size of the Navy, or even a large rise in the size of the Navy, gives you more students to train, admittedly, but you do this over a period of time. It just doesn't happen right that day. But your resources are increased proportionately to the very rapid increase in the size of the Navy. You take advantage, then, of this situation by doing some of the things, or putting aside some of the resources to do those things that you haven't been able to do up to this point. I'll give you an example in a little bit of what I have in mind in this linear effect.

Right at the present time we in the training establishment are endeavoring to take steps to convince the powers that be that the linear formula is not one that really should be applied to the education and training situation, especially when navy strength is going down.

Q: Has it always applied?

Mr. K.: In my experience it has always applied in some form, although you didn't necessarily find everyone willing to admit that that was what was going on. But you obviously got your cuts just as if someone had taken a slide rule and figured out your proportion, and you were told, therefore, this is what you can have. Then you operated within the confines of what you were given to operate with. So it's always been there and it's there today to a degree in a computer system which has been created by the research agencies of the Navy. The Navy's training establishment is fighting against the application of this linear reduction. However, we're suffering rather extensively at this stage of the game in what amounts to a linear reduction--being told this is how many you will reduce, this is the rate at which you will cut down. Therefore, the application even today is on a linear basis, whether it's right or not.

Q: I think you were about to give me a specific--

Mr. K.: Let me go on here a little bit and then I'll come to that specific example.

The Navy depends almost entirely on its own talented people in uniform to serve as instructors. This has been good. The Navy has developed its own instructors and instructor training schools, and they've been effective. They're also dedicated, and that helps. Civilian educational specialists have been used in support of training. Some are used to teach, but their function has been limited primarily to guiding the Navy uniformed instructors and in assuring that the best in pedagogical techniques, materials, and subject matter was employed.

Q: The Naval Academy is an exception to that? To the military being the teaching staff?

Mr. K.: There are military who do teach at the Naval Academy, but the Naval Academy is unique in the sense that when George Bancroft established the Naval Academy he looked around for a faculty and it came out, I think, that three out of the first seven instructors he selected were civilians. And approximately this ratio has been maintained over the years. But it differs from the other military academies who do not use civilians to nearly the same degree.

In most of its teaching the Navy has maintained a teaching force which is made up of the seagoing people who come back to shore duty and who have the knowledge, the technical knowledge, necessary but are not necessarily good instructors. The problem, therefore, is to improve their capability to deliver from a platform and be instructors. We have a few civil service instructors in the electronics field. We have made some very sparse efforts in the direction of civilianizing our instructional force. It hasn't worked out very well in most instances. One of the things we learned very soon after we went to contracting for instructors was that the contractor was employing, for the most part, people who had just gotten out of the Navy or the Army or the Air Force. If we could just figure out a way to keep those people in uniform, why, we wouldn't have to pay the contractor to go out and hire them!

The training establishment has been continually in competition with other elements for the construction of suitable facilities. At the time of the advent of World War II, training facilities were sparse. They consisted principally of the buildings at the United States Naval Academy constructed at various times, from the early years of the twentieth century--some buildings at Great Lakes were built in 1911, others at San Diego were built in 1928. Consequently most training facilities after World War II were temporary wooden structures built to last only five years or so. So some buildings that were built for other purposes were obtained from civilian sources.

The story is told of the construction of a recruit training facility at Great Lakes, wherein a foresighted, energetic Public Works officer had building construction people working on the site the day after Pearl Harbor. An example of the use of civilian discarded facilities is the naval postgraduate school, and here I come to that example that I was going to use, to show how one takes advantage of the linear effect of an increasing navy endstrength.

The Delmonte Hotel at Monterey had been taken over by the Navy in World War II for the purpose of training enlisted men in basic electronics. After the war it was available, and its civilian proprietors were evidently glad to sell it to the government. The Navy first established there a unit of the five-term program designed to make professional career officers out of the officers who came into the Navy in World War II who did not possess a baccalaureate degree. Monterey and Newport provided the professional naval aspects. They received their academic education and their degrees from civilian colleges.

The relocation of the postgraduate school from Annapolis, where it started in 1909 as an adjunct of the U. S. Naval Academy, makes an interesting story. It was at the time of the Korean incident and the Navy was building up for that effort.

Early one morning the then PersC, who was Captain, later Rear Admiral George C. "Bull" Towner, came in to chat, as he often did. He said, "Prent, last night I had a real good idea. We've been trying for some time to get better facilities for our PG school in Annapolis through the military construction program. Why don't we pick it up and move it to Monterey? We could do it during the Christmas leave period."

This sounded like a good idea to me, and to make a longer story shorter, that is what we did, building Butler Buildings for classroom and lab spaces with money made temporarily more plentiful by the international crisis.

Q: And you met no objection to this?

Mr. K.: Well, we really didn't wait for any. We just advised the postgraduate school people that they were going to move and the people at Monterey that we were going to send them some money to build some Butler buildings with or buy some buildings and set them up. They went right along with it. This is what I was trying to indicate before, that in periods of crisis you have a lot more latitude than you have in normal times or in times when the Navy is being decreased. Therefore, this is the time when you'd better be foresighted and get in there, get what you can and accomplish those things that you haven't been able to accomplish before.

Q: But then you have the problem of holding on to these advances in leaner times?

Mr. K.: Well, you have now established a plateau from which you now are going to be cut, rather than being cut from the lower plateau that you would have been on if you hadn't had the crisis! So, yes, you suffer. You have to find out now what it is you're going to do away with and some of those things may be things that you have just decided are real high priority. This is all a matter of management of the training organization.

The story does not end there, of course, because the postgraduate school now possesses in addition to the old hotel many new engineering classrooms and lab spaces, both on the main campus and on the auxiliary landing field. There is a new library, several-hundred family housing units, and, last but not least, an 18-hole golf course. It is now one of the nation's outstanding graduate schools and the civilian professors there are paid salaries which rate among the top salaries of the nation's educational world.

Even the U. S. Naval Academy has been practically rebuilt in the last twenty-five years. To those who might say I was a midshipman in Bancroft Hall in the 1920s and it is still there, I would assert that Bancroft Hall was almost completely rebuild inside at a cost of about $30 million and now has some added wings. The Naval Academy still has some old structures which will be replaced in future years. But Michelson-Chauvenet Hall and the new $26-million-dollar engineering complex now being constructed are and will be marvels of the military academic world.

Great Lakes still has a way to go before it is totally rebuilt, and likewise NTC, San Diego, still has some old buildings. But the expenditure of many millions has succeeded in making these installations ones in which the Navy can take pride.

Perhaps one of the most notable achievements in the facilities area is the construction at Orlando, Florida, of the Navy's third recruit training center. This was constructed on the newest design and is probably the nation's only recruit training center built completely from scratch as a recruit training center, including in-processing facilities, an outstanding chapel, a fire-fighting school with an afterburner, anti-smoke-pollution device, a first on a new structure, and a dispensary with dental facilities. It's cost, so far, about $70 million.

Q: Let me ask, did you have any trouble getting the funds from Congress for these additions and new buildings and what have you?

Mr. K.: Yes, we always have trouble.

Q: Jack Chew tells me it's much easier to get a chapel than it is some other things.

Mr. K.: I think this goes in cycles. I've been there many times, been through the wringer many times when we were trying for chapels and we would come away without a single chapel. We've been trying, for example, to get one out at Monterey at the postgraduate school for at least ten years and we haven't got it yet.

Right at the minute hospitals are the Number One item. You can sell Congress, it seems, on a hospital when you can't sell them anything else, especially if it's in the chairman's district!

Q: I suppose they're hospital-conscious because of a war going on?

Mr. K.: Well, this is one reason, but another thing is that Navy hospitals--I think particularly naval hospitals--got pretty far behind the curve, they got to be in pretty bad shape.

Q: Chelsea?

Mr. K.: Right. Chelsea is one of the ones that's thrown up as a shining example. These are the kinds of things that go in cycles. Another thing that can be sold today pretty readily is housing. I don't mean public housing for officers and families. That sells, but bachelor enlisted quarters, and officer BOQs are pretty good salable articles these days.

Training has had its ups and downs and sometimes things sell better than other times. But you always have your difficulties, you are almost always bound, in my experience, to lose something out of the programs when they get to the Congress. Some of this results because of the fact that the Congress says to the Navy, what's your priority list, we're in the business of cutting things, so we're obviously going to cut something. So what order do you want these things arranged in? In recent years the Navy has put housing high on the list and they have put medical facilities high on the list, and so when it got to training you were apt to find training appearing, at least some projects of it, in the lower 20 percent. Not because they had anything against training but other things were awarded a higher place on the Navy's priority list. You give 80 percent to these other things, you see, and you don't have much left with which to build training facilities. So we've lost a lot of things over the years. But, to continue with the Orlando story. Orlando was an Air Force base which was located adjacent to what is now Herndon Airfield, which was turned over to the city of Orlando. The Orlando story is an interesting one. The Navy had three large training centers at the end of World War II. These were Great Lakes, Bainbridge, and San Diego.

In 1957 a budget squeeze prompted the closing of Bainbridge. Experience after that time demonstrated overcrowing, meningitis, and other difficulties that three recruit camps were essential. BuPers wanted to rebuild Bainbridge and got support for plans to that end at high Navy and OSD levels and proceeded in that direction. Actually, a new building for Bainbridge was authorized before 1957 but construction was blocked by the Bureau of the Budget which thought the Navy was going to get smaller. Later, Congress authorized and funded a new recruit barracks for women which was build and which the women recruits recently abandoned when they were moved to Orlando in the summer of 1972, not into new buildings for women recruits, as planned, but into a converted male recruit building.

The plan for rebuilding Bainbridge was aborted when Under SecNav Baldwin was convinced by an OSD rep that Bainbridge was not a good place to train recruits--too cold for outdoor training and besides Bainbridge was a good place to relocate some Washington activities from Washington, since getting out of Washington was a game being played then, as now.

Q: Navy activities?

Mr. K.: Not necessarily Navy activities, because this

individual in OSD had responsibility for all the military services, so he might be influential in getting something else out of Washington. Bainbridge was nearby, you see, and offered an opportunity to put something there that was then in Washington. So Secretary Baldwin directed BuPers to find a site in southeast USA.

We found Orlando, which had been looked at before for a number of purposes. One of the two takes on the Orlando Navy property is now called Lake Baldwin!

It is not intended to be disparaging of how things work in the government, but rather to illustrate how they work. Another example worthy of mention into which political influence entered was the relocation of the Navy Supply Corps School from Bayonne, New Jersey, to Athens, Georgia. I was away from my office one afternoon in the early 1950s when my front office called to say that Chairman Carl Vinson of the House Armed Services Committee had called to "suggest" the Navy become interested in acquiring some real estate used by the University of Georgia at Athens. I was instructed to proceed post haste to Athens, which I did with two officers, one Supply Corps and one general line.

To describe a long and pleasant experience briefly, we came, we saw, and we bought the girls' school portion of an old normal school at the University of Georgia and moved the officer Supply School from Bayonne, New Jersey, where it was located in sad facilities, to Athens into facilities that really were not much better, since some of the structures had been built before the Civil War.

Q: In deference to the same gentleman you located something at Milledgeville, didn't you?

Mr. K.: The Navy didn't. That was some other branch of the military. We never had training at Milledgeville.

However, construction facilities came much easier in Georgia in those days than they did any place else. So it was a good investment, even though Athens is a long way from any salt water. Several new buildings have been constructed, others are being constructed, and many units of family housing are in place.

Of course, buying real estate for which the University of Georgia wanted several millions of dollars was not easy for the Navy, but it was easy for Congressman Vinson. The Navy had not programmed any funds and it was not in the DOD-approved military construction program. Vice Admiral L. T. Dubose, then the Chief of Naval Personnel, who also hailed from Georgia, made this clear to the congressional committee. However, Chairman Vinson explained to the committee that the Navy had a real need, that Athens was not in his district, but that the Georgia property would be a bargain for the Navy since he himself had told the University authorities that, although they were asking much more, 2.5 million dollars was all he would recommend. The Chairman then proposed the insertion of a new item in the construction program and the committee members duly made it so.

So that is how the Navy acquired its very nice Supply Corps School in Athens, Georgia.

I recall one other similar significant move of a facility. We had looked for a place to relocate the Navy Communications Technicians School, then at Imperial Beach, California in horrible facilities. We had favored Corona, California where the Navy still owned the property, a hotel converted to a large hospital in World War II, and had looked also at the Mare Island ex-naval hospital. These are West Coast sites. Corona was really too large and the old hospital wings at Mare Island didn't lend themselves to economical classroom utilization. About that time the Navy was retrenching at Pensacola and Corey Field was to be closed.

Congressman Robert Sikes "persuaded" the Navy to move its CT school from Imperial Beach, California, to Pensacola, Florida. The classroom buildings at Corey were provided by converting large airplane hangars, which by the way make real good classroom buildings, at a cost, of course. Much building has since been accomplished at Corey Field and much more is in sight. It also was a good move.

As we have noted, Navy training often has been compelled to use facilities built for something else. We now use, for example, the old Mare Island Naval Hospital as a nucleus for a much-expanded guided missile automatic data processing combat weapons training facility. Corey Field was an auxiliary naval air station. The postgraduate school was the Delmonte Hotel. The Naval Training Center at Orlando was a discarded Air Force base. However, the Navy has made good use of what was usable and in each case has succeeded in getting good functional facilities. Housing, messing, and support facilities have also improved immensely over the past thirty years. The area of facilities being more tangible and also having had the support of powerful congressmen, it is one where we can see and appreciate much gain.

Q: In this same area, I have a question. I think it pertains in this area. You mentioned before one of the schools, I guess the PG school, where students got degrees from private colleges and universities and I know that the Naval War College has had an arrangement with George Washington University for the awarding of degrees. Does all of this come under the cognizance of Navy Personnel?

Mr. K.: The matter of degrees and the granting of them has been a function of the training organization in the Navy, and, of course, when it was BuPers, it was a BuPers responsibility. These various programs that you mention have to be identified in two different categories.

One, the Navy does send naval officers to civilian educational institutions. This is usually when the Navy doesn't have in its graduate school a particular kind of instruction that you can get in civilian educational institutions. Therefore, we send people to graduate schools, some forty or so different institutions and among them, just as an example, is the training and advanced education for chaplains. They don't teach religion at the graduate school, the Navy's postgraduate school, so therefore, we send Navy chaplains to get their education.

Q: Where do they go?

Mr. K.: They go to various schools. George Washington University, Yale, are among those that I recall offhand, but there are many different institutions where they are sent, usually at the option of the Chief of Chaplains as to where he would like to have his people go or where the people themselves would like to go.

I mentioned moving the postgraduate school out to Monterey and the five-term program being there already. This was an undergraduate program and was designed to take the Reserve officers who elected to remain in the Navy who had not acquired baccalaureate degrees, and send them to a civilian institution to get their academic background and a baccalaureate degree. And also at the same time and in the same evolution to put them through what were called the general-line schools so that they got a background-- the same kind of professional background that the Naval Academy graduates got by going to the Naval Academy.

Q: Does the Navy have a voice in the class structure, course structure, in a civilian institution when they send men there?

Mr. K.: Not as a usual thing. We send them there for the purpose of getting a particular specialization that that school furnishes or to get a degree, like the undergraduate people. You would buy whatever the institution had in its catalogue. However, by contract the Navy does acquire tailored courses in civilian institutions.

For example, George Washington University teaches naval fiscal management. It's a course which was evolved by the Navy, but the University furnishes under contract the instructional force and talent to conduct it.

Q: Civilians?

Mr. K.: Yes, a civilian faculty. Then, of course, any degree that you get by that means is granted by the institution. We have another arrangement, for example, at the present time with the University of Rochester to teach naval and officers from the other armed services what's called "defense systems management." This is a fifteen-months course and it's conducted in collaboration with the Center for Naval Analysis here in Washington. That is a tailored course that does not exist or isn't given anywhere else by any other institution. Therefore, it's done under special contract with the University of Rochester.

So you have lots of latitude to go and buy what's on the shelf or change it if you don't like what you see on the shelf and make it more suitable for your purposes.

Q: I suppose the courses offered at MIT, at least those I know about just before World War II under Dr. Draper, were they contractual arrangements?

Mr. K.: The Navy has been sending people to MIT for as long as I can remember. In the main the Navy is sending individuals to MIT to take what courses MIT offers. The selection of courses is, of course, left to, or influenced largely by the individual or by the command that he is being trained to take a place in. What used to be the Bureau of Ships--now the Ships Systems Command--for example, had a very large interest in the courses at MIT that provided people versed in shipbuilding pursuits.

Q: Naval constructors!

Mr. K.: Yes, Sir. There's a naval constrction course, it used to be called.

This kind of regulation of what courses the individual will take is a function of the postgraduate school, which communicates with the institution and with the officers who are going to the institution and keeps track of them. It maintains a staff at Monterey for the purpose of doing this.

Well, I'll now get ahead with my outline and talk a little bit about what I call characteristics of Navy education and training.

CHARACTERISTICS OF NAVY EDUCATION AND TRAINING

We have already noted that from the beginning Navy training was practical, most often on the job and designed to prepare the Navy man to do the job. Even though his instruction might be commonly termed education he was really in training for the naval profession in the same sense that medical training prepares a doctor of medicine. Training moved ashore only when the technical requirements demanded some theoretical background and understanding of the operational and maintenance responsibilities. For many years the Navy insisted that it trained ashore only in those pursuits which experience indicated were not well accomplished by the on-the-job method. This is still a fundamental premise in that plans for advancing personnel in rating assume that certain numbers, the percentage depending on the complexity of the specialty, acquire their needed skills and knowledge through on-the-job training and will not require shore-based training.

However, more recently a new need for training has entered the picture. This, simply said, is the need for using training as an incentive for re-enlistment and officer procurement and retention. This need resulted in the granting of educational training opportunities to deserving individuals in exchange for extended or new periods of active duty. The number of such programs is large. I would mention only a couple.

One of these was the Navy Enlisted Scientific Education Program developed as far back as 1956. It was initially envisioned as an advanced training enlistment incentive. It soon became and still is an officer-procurement program which gives deserving enlisted men a chance to acquire a college education and a degree in a scientific or engineering specialty and a naval officer commission after going through the officer candidate school. A participant acquires a substantial obligation for continued active service in exchange for the education.

Q: Has this truly proved effective in increasing the re-enlistment?

Mr. K.: It's difficult to judge the extent to which it has had an influence on re-enlistment, but it is held up as one of the Navy's efforts in the direction of being good to enlisted people. I'm sure that it has prompted many people to make application for the program and many people have been accepted for the program. We actually are putting in to the NESEP program right now about 400 a year. Therefore, it is one of the incentives that provides interest among the enlisted people in the fleet. Not all of them can qualify to go to college, of course--

Q: I was about to ask, is it entirely optional on their part or is there a process of elimination?

Mr. K.: It's optional insofar as application is concerned. They have to meet certain standards and one of the more important standards is the assessment by the man't commanding officer. In other words, he has to be recommended by his commanding officer. We get several thousand applications, of course, and this gets weeded down by a process, which is primarily one of whether or not it looks as if the individual could scholastically carry college work. So the screening is primarily on the basis, not of limiting the numbers, but of finding those who are willing and anxious and who qualify.

Q: And the schools are designated?

Mr. K.: The schools are designated and carry on under contract. With few exceptions, the schools selected, of which there are about twenty, are schools which have NROTC units. This obviously is because it is an economy in not having to have a separate staff there to administer the students. The individual is kept within bounds insofar as the kind of subject matter that he can take is concerned. It is a way in which the Navy has pulled itself up by its bootstraps largely in the scientific and engineering fields. Obviously you can get lots of people who have had baccalaureate training to volunteer for the Navy but success in getting engineering types and scientists has not been so good. So this is one of the means by which you overcome the difficulty.

To answer your question another way, has the program been good for the Navy? I would say yes, I think it's been one of the more outstanding educational efforts. It's one which is looked upon very highly by the Congress, commended actually by congressional committee. The other services have looked at it with a good deal of envy, but so far don't have anything that exactly resembles it.

Another program is the Associate Degree Completion Program, which is called ADCOP. This was designed to encourage enlisted personnel to extend their periods of active duty using a junior college associate degree as bait. This program was deliberately aimed at keeping enlisted men in enlisted status, while improving their technical ability and retaining their talents over a longer period. In other words, the NESEP program quickly grew into what amounts to an officer-procurement program and our problem was how do you keep technically qualified enlisted men as enlisted men.

We now have in the ADCOP program several hundred. We have perhaps as many as 2,000 enlisted men who are enrolled in about twelve or fourteen different junior colleges around the country. This also has proved to be a real good incentive because the individual has to qualify, make good while he's in school, learn something that will be good for him when he comes back to his job, and he also acquires an obligated service for the education that he received. Therefore, you now have an individual who's been in the Navy long enough to be selected for this kind of program and you send him to school. The average length of time is about seventeen months. Then you have him for a protracted period beyond that and by that time he's built up enough equity in Navy service so that you're pretty sure you're going to hang on to him for a career.

Q: In connection with this program, is any consideration given to the wife in the case, if there is a wife?

Mr. K.: Only in that she accompanies the student, of course, as does the entire family, if there is a family, to the educational site and has the opportunity of taking courses. Up to now, anyway, these courses would be on her own.

There are many efforts made not only in these campus educational programs to bring the wives into the picture, by having coffees and teas and social events which do include the wives. They are given orientation lectures at the beginning, which are designed to tell the wife what her part is in the program, that the husband is going to be really working pretty hard, and she can help by encouraging him and keeping him going forward in the right direction.

Q: This is a psychological factor, then?

Mr. K.: And a real worthwhile one. Of course, the Navy has carried out many of these programs on a large scale by the creation of wives clubs and that type of thing, bringing the wives into the program, you might say.

As the military establishment faces, as it does today, the all-volunteer force concept and educational and training incentives are being looked upon with increasing favor. But this adds to the problem of the training establishment as it faces drastic curtailment in resources along with other facets of the Navy.

Q: May I ask you to hark back for a question--the contrast between the results obtained in on-the-job training--the contrast with on-shore training, has a study been made of that ever?

Mr. K.: Yes. Lots of research has been done on this and the results can be summarized by saying that most everything that is taught by Navy schools can be learned by on-the-job methods. However, the speed at which one acquires the knowledge is much greater in school, in a formalized training program. Still, you do look to training on the job in many areas. For example, in the case of boatswainmates, there are no schools on shore. All the training is done at sea on the job. So one of the best measures of this kind of thing is the nation-wide, or world-wide, examination system of enlisted personnel. Examinations are given for a single specialty all over the world, on board all ships on the same day. The people who are allowed to take these examinations include those who have gone through school and those who have received what training they received by on-the-job methods. You find in the studies that you make of the statistics which you gather this way that some people who have been trained on the job do pretty well in these examinations. So you take this factor into consideration when you establish the school quotas. In other words, if you found by this examination process that a fifth of the people who had passed the examination got their training by on-the-job methods, then you can assume that in the future a fifth will also get their knowledge by that method, so you regulate the school input quotas accordingly.

This is one of the best measures that I know of for determining what the relationship is. Some ratings, of course, are almost 100 percent trained in school. Electronics technicians would naturally be one of these. The training of parachute riggers is another one where the Navy doesn't take a chance on in-service or on-the-job training. You have to go to school to be a parachute rigger--

Q: Learn some of the essentials before you try it!

Mr. K.: Right--and the medical profession, what we used to call the corpsman, and the dental technician, are required to go to school before they're allowed to enter into anything on the job. This doesn't mean that they aren't going to learn on the job later, but their fundamental training takes place in schools.

Q: I was thinking primarily of on-the-job training aboard ship, where you have a self-contained unit removed from the blandishments of ordinary life, perhaps concentration would be greater? The application?

Mr. K.: The application of on-the-job training, you mean?

Q: Yes.

Mr. K.: This is true, and a lot of it goes on. Of course, I wouldn't want to leave anyone with the impression that school training and the training that the individual gets in school qualifies a man to undertake every job that he faces when he gets aboard ship. He's still going to be learning. The objective of the school has been to give him the fundamentals so that he can learn by reading a blueprint or reading the words in a manual and following through. In other words, he has had some acquaintanceship with the terminology at least and, in the cast of electronics technicians, the concept of what an electron is and what it does under certain circumstances. So then he can read the literature with some understanding, which he otherwise wouldn't be able to do.

Q: What about correspondence courses?

Mr. K.: The Navy carries on what has been claimed to be the world's largest correspondence course program. There are a number of agencies, one of which is the Naval War College which is engaged in the correspondence course program. But the majority of correspondence courses are administered by the Naval Correspondence Course Center which is located in Scotia, New York. It has the responsibility for assembling the correspondence course itself, which may not be prepared at Scotia, and sending it out to the various ships. In the case of enlisted personnel, the correspondence courses are corrected on board ship. In the case of officers, they're sent back to Scotia and corrected there. The Correspondence Course Center at Scotia dispenses and processes something on the order of about 1.2 million courses a year. These are available to Reserves as well as to regular active duty people.

There's an incentive for the enlisted personnel, particularly, to take correspondence courses, because as a part of their advancement in rating process they have to be able to certify, or have certified for them, that they have taken the correspondence course which is designed to suit their backgrounds and improve their capabilities before they're allowed to take the examination.

Q: So it's truly advisable to do this as one advancement?

Mr. K.: It's truly an incentive.

Q: What about the individual educational programs I've heard about from time to time on single units in the fleet, say, the aircraft carrier would engage in a fairly comprehensive educational program under the aegis of the skipper? Is this inspired by Washington?

Mr. K.: I think you might say that. As Navy Regulations specify, and I guess it was John Paul Jones who stated this first--the responsibility of a skipper is to train his crew. Therefore, it's written down in the law, you might say, that this is one of the responsibilities. Obviously, his attention is devoted in large measure to being sure that his crew assembles at the right place and is able to fire a gun or be engaged in "man overboard" drill and that sort of thing, but also each ship and each command has an educational officer He usually has this function as additional duty. His function is to promote among the members of the crew the opportunities that are available through correspondence courses, through going to school on shore, whether it's for a short course of half a day or half a year. So there is a continual process that is employed in any command in assuring that its personnel are aware of and are encouraged to accept the opportunities that are available for them to improve themselves.

There is an OpNav directive on so-called general military training, which instructs with regard to the responsibilities of the individual commanding officers as to what his responsibilities are in various areas. There are some 28 areas, as I remember last reading. So he therefore has pressure, if you wish. But on the whole I think it's the kind of thing that any dedicated commanding officer, or any people manager, would be pushing on as hard as he can to assure that his crew members are aware of their opportunities and accept them.

Q: I was particularly impressed with the scope of some of these programs that have to do with background in the history of the country they're going to visit, the concept that each and every man on board is a representative of the United States when he goes ashore, and something about local customs and what's expected of him as a representative of our government and so forth. None of this then is inspired from Washington?

Mr. K.: Oh, yes. Much of that, as a matter of fact. I can give you an individual who has been in the forefront of that kind of thing, that overseas indoctrination. His name is Dave Rosenberg, who has had a very varied and interesting career. Many years ago he became interested in this matter of indoctrination of individuals who were going to other countries. I'm not sure how his interest was motivated, but he, among other things, is a very expert folk dancer. He engages with the recreational authorities here in the District of Columbia in folk dancing and teaches folk dancing, and so on. So he had become interested in foreign lands and foreign nations, I think probably through his folk dancing. In other words, what kind of dances do they have? In the Bureau of Naval Personnel, he was a member of the Pers C staff, and, as I say, on his own volition mainly he became very much interested and enthusiastic. He sold the program pretty much by himself, was given a real small team to go around and visit the ships before they went to South America or went to Europe, and we sent him all over the Far East to learn the customs and so on, and bring it back and set up a program.

He has made at least one film and maybe a series of films that show him going through the processes by which he brings this indoctrination to the people going overseas. He's still in Washington. That was one of the programs, however, that when we left BuPers we left in BuPers, so he is operating from there now. He gets a kind of Washington push, if you wish, by making his services avaiable. He was a real popular individual, with lots of calls from high-ranking officers about to depart to overseas, you know. "How about sending Dave down? We need him real badly." We were pretty well pressed many times to find the resources to get him there and get him back. He could make a fascinating story all by himself.

I mentioned that in this era of the all-volunteer force we're being pressured in the training organization to provide more incentives so that people will be interested in coming in the Navy and staying in the Navy when they get in under voluntary circumstances, rather than driven by the draft. One of the areas that the Navy presently has under development in this connection is a very ambitious program which is called the "Navy Campus for Achievement."

This program has the purpose of promoting educational opportunities or incentives, particularly for enlisted men who may be motivated toward acqusition of a baccalaureate degree. Two new features are significent. We've had various programs, of course, designed in that direction, but this program in the first place has a purpose of accumulation of academic records and credit for individuals throughout the Navy into a single computer so that a continuous record of each participant's progress is immediately available. The second motivation or objective is active cooperation on the part of certain civilian universities who will agree to grant college credit toward a degree on the basis of work in Navy schools, other colleges, examinations, and other sources. A competent corps of educational advisers located strategically in areas of fleet concentration is visualized. This program is sometimes referred to as "the college without walls." It is currently receiving much emphasis within the Navy.

Q: Who gave birth to that idea?

Mr. K.: Well, the idea really has been one of long standing, and we have had some little success in getting into this arena. When I say "some success" we have had some contractual arrangements with the U. S. International University, which has its headquarters in San Diego and which has been promoting institutions around the world. Unfortunately, the ones that they have so far including one in London and one in Athens, have not been where there are Navy concentrations.

Q: We're about to have one in Athens!

Mr. K.: We're about to have some people in Athens anyway. So we've had a little experience. We've had some negotiations with various institutions, including a Colorado University. Since Admiral Cagle has come into the fold he has taken a particularly outstanding and personal interest in promoting this kind of thing. He has gained acquaintance with many of the educational authorities, particularly in the Pensacola and University of Florida educational system, and is promoting it very much personally. He has just now brought back on active duty a retired admiral, maybe you knew him, James Lloyd "Doc" Abbot, who is heading up a new unit in Pensacola. He's called the Director of Educational Development, and this Campus for Achievement is going to be one of the important features, I'm sure, as long as Admiral Cagle is there, of the operation of the unit.

Q: Cagle may have been reluctant to take over this job originally, but he seems to have—

Mr. K.: Well, you know Admiral Cagle. He's an enthusiast. Those things that he gets enthusiastic for, he goes at in a real dedicated way. This is one of the things that's dear to his heart.

One of the things that has happened recently that my office has some relationship to is what used to be called the Secretary's Advisory Board for Educational Requirements (SABER). There was a period when it wasn't doing much of anything. Admiral Cagle has been instrumental in rejuvenating it and now it's called SABET, Secretary's Advisory Board for Education and Training. This is a group of leading citizens, educators in large measure, but not limited to educators, that he is getting together. They've had one meeting so far in late November, and another one in Pensacola in the middle of February, 1973. He's bringing in the educational fraternity, you might say, to sit down and talk about some of these things. One of his primary motivations, I'm sure, is that he is trying to work up enthusiasm in the academic world for joining up with the Navy in this business of providing academic credits. Even though the student didn't go to your school, boys, we'd like to have you join up with us. Resources for this program, which will be considerable, have got to come, I'm sure, by relatively small steps and re-programming from resources which may be available. So it's going to be an interesting project and a worthwhile one, I'm sure, but not one that will be consummated next week and probably not next year either.

Interview No. 3 with Mr. Prent Kenyon

Place: His office in Arlington, Virginia

Date: Wednesday afternoon, 21 February 1973

Subject: Biography

By: John T. Mason, Jr.

Q: It's mighty good to see you again today. I'm sorry you have a cold but you share, I suppose, the experience of half of mankind at this point!

There were a couple of questions I wanted to ask covering largely the material you dealt with last time, or additions to it. I'm cognizant of the fact that in World War II various schools were set up, one in particular out in Colorado to facilitate the teaching of Japanese and so forth. Did Personnel have some cognizance there?

Mr. K.: Yes, they were Bureau of Personnel training activities. Primarily language courses of considerable length were taught in civilian institutions, such as Colorado. Usually this was for the purpose of training the security types who were going to go overseas to be in strategic places and who needed to have a real good knowledge of the language of the country that they were about to visit. After the war, the Navy set up in Anacostia here in Washington an intelligence school which had as a part of it a language section. This came to take the place of schools which were at the collegiate level or established in connection with colleges during World War II. The intelligence school and its language section really operated as a part of the postgraduate school and had the capability of employing faculty members under the same rules, for example, as the postgraduate school did. The Navy in later years was persuaded to give up its intelligence school and its language school and turn them over to the DOD schools, intelligence school and language schools, so that the Navy language school then became part of the Defense Language Institute, which provides today most of the language training--that is, long-term language training--that is provided for all the armed services.

Q: I would assume that the Army had made a similar effort and you were simply combining forces under the Department of Defense?

Mr. K.: Yes, each of the three services had some language, although the Navy was actually the only one that had what you might consider a formal language school. It, therefore, formed the basis for the foundation for the Defense Language Institute, and the Navy facilities were actually used for a long time by the Defense Language Institute.

Q: During World War II when this language school was set up in Colorado, what sort of cooperation did BuPers extend to ONI, which was in the vanguard of this effort?

Mr. K.: Well, ONI along with the security group people

were, of course, customers of the language training programs which were supported by the training organization of the Navy.

I should say, parenthetically, though, in connection with my previous information that the Army did have and the Defense Language Institute still has a unit out in Monterey, California, of fairly considerable size insofar as language instruction is concerned.

Q: Inasmuch as you mention Monterey, you did say last time that they were running into various problems with the school there, but you didn't enumerate those problems. Do you want to talk about that?

Mr. K.: I'm not sure that I remember too well the problems that we had. The graduate school has had problems over the years in obtaining sufficient facilities, but in recent years I think the Navy has done pretty well in providing them with facilities at Monterey in the postgraduate school. This is different from the language school, which is at the Presidio, the Army's installation at Monterey. They're close by each other, but they're not the same thing.

The facilities at the postgraduate school have come along real well in recent years. We would like to have pretty soon now an ocean sciences building or buildings. Two of them are in the program, but in general I think the postgraduate school has been faring pretty well.

Q: From time to time, officers have told me that somewhere along in their career they have consulted with BuPers and have enrolled for graduate education, paying their own fees. Is this a rare thing?

Mr. K.: The Navy in recent years has had a number of different programs in which the individual has paid either part of the fees or all of them, depending upon what his status might be and how many years he still has to do in the Navy. The Navy, of course, along with the other services, has had a tuition aid program in being for many years in which the individual is financed up to 75 percent of the tuition cost for courses which he takes in an off-duty status. More recently the Navy has chosen a limited number not to exceed 50 each year of officers who are interested in applying for the opportunity to go back to college and get a degree or a more advanced degree, and in these instances the Navy pays the individual's salary as if he were, and he is, still on active duty. But he pays his own tuition and college fees.

Q: I was thinking particularly of Admiral Chick Hayward, whom you know. He told me that at one stage in his career he couldn't get any backing from the Navy for advanced education, so he went out on his own and did it.

Mr. K.: I'm sure there are a lot of officers who have gone out in years past. One of the difficulties that the Navy has experienced just recently is trying to get tabs on all of those people who have taken courses on their own and who have got degrees or advanced degrees on their own and who, therefore, have now become a part of the inventory of educated officers. Sometimes this gets held against us because the Office of Management and Budget and OSD and the Congress find that the Navy's got more officers with degrees in certain pursuits than the Navy has requirements for. So it became a give-and-take proposition in which the Navy attempts to use, as best it can, the educational talents which have been acquired by officers, whether they did it on their own or how they got it.

Q: I know a few of them. I think a primary example is Admiral Dennison, who has now retired, of course, but he went on and got his Ph.D. at Johns Hopkins on his own, while he was serving in Annapolis.

Mr. K.: Yes. Up until the last five or six years I think that, except through the Navy's graduate education program, which was specifically designed to educate people to do a Navy job, if an individual got advanced education, why, he got it because he was ambitious enough to go out and get it for himself. But things have changed now and the Navy has come to be more favorably inclined toward education. Therefore, it is at least contributing to a degree and the direction of the ambitious of the individuals.

Q: That leads me to another example in the person of Chuck Merdinger, who was a Rhodes Scholar. He felt that the Navy really frowned on men being selected as Rhodes Scholars. He said that it has changed now since World War II, but up to that time he thought there was something of a roadblock!

Mr. K.: Well, the history of scholarships, Rhodes or otherwise, has been cyclic. There have been times when those in charge were inclined in the direction of getting maximum work out of the talent that was available and therefore not looking toward the opportunities to let people go to school on a scholarship basis or otherwise. But more recently the Navy has come to have a very liberal attitude towards scholarships, so therefore, any officer who can obtain a scholarship from any legitimate institution is authorized to go and collect, and in many cases the Navy will support the scholarship by either paying the man's salary, if that's required, or paying his travel expenses as may be necessary so that he can accept the Rhodes scholarship.

So there are quite a few people now who are engaged in education on scholarships.

Q: Mr. Kenyon, you said the other day, when you were talking about the campus for achievement, you talked about the method of keeping track of academic credits and records being computerized. I wondered if this is going to result in more adequate assignments for a person, if their achievements in this area will be fitted to the kind of jobs to which they're assigned?

Mr. K.: I would find that difficult to answer definitively. I would think that the more information that's available to the detailer, the more chance there is that he'll detail a round peg into a round hole. However, there are a lot of other considerations, and so this answer doesn't really come out to be either black or white.

The Bureau of Naval Personnel has taken some real enlightened steps recently in the direction of detailing enlisted men by name and directly from Washington. Accordingly, a record which would show the individual's accumulation of academic credits would be all to the good in the direction of giving that centralized detailer the opportunity of knowing more about the man than he otherwise would know. This, of course, is one of the things that's being taken into consideration as attention is being given these days to what kind of an academic record they're going to have.

I would say yes, it ought to at least provide the information that's not now readily available.

Q: Sir, of late we've heard a great deal about minorities and so forth in the Navy, is there any specific program directed toward minorities to bring their educational accomplishments and standards up to par with some others?

Mr. K.: Yes, the Navy has tried hard in several different directions in this connection to overcome the cultural background or lack of it of certain individuals. An example of this would be the Better Opportunities For Officer Selection And Training, (BOOST) Program, which was originally set up in Bainbridge, Maryland, but has since been shifted to San Diego, California. This is a program specially designed to pick out those people who are found in the Navy who have been culturally deprived and, therefore, have not had educational opportunities that they might otherwise have had. Of course, on the order of 90 percent of those who have entered the training so far have been black. The design, the ambition, of this program is to provide up to two years of academic background for these individuals so that they will have the opportunity to be selected for the NROTC program or the Naval Academy and given an opportunity to go to those officer-training programs.

Q: Is it also being used as an inducement for re-enlistments?

Mr. K.: I don't know that we can attribute anything in the way of race and culturally deprived aspects, that we have anything in that area which is designed to get re-enlistments. The Navy, of course, does have a lot of inducements these days and there are coming to be more and more. The tuition-aid program, for example. The associate-degree-completion program which permits enlisted personnel to go to school and get an associate degree. All of these are designed as incentives. We've mentioned the campus for achievement which will be used as a means of encouraging Navy people to enlist and re-enlist in the Navy.

In addition to the BOOST Program, insofar as race relations are concerned, which, of course, is a subject very paramount at the minute, the Navy from the top down has instituted various kinds of instructional seminars and human relations efforts of various kinds. A great deal of effort and a great many resources are being devoted at this time to the endeavor to obtain understanding on the part of the Navy leaders and middle management of the human rights and human relationships of the individuals with whom they come in contact. This is a program of great emphasis which has come on down from on high, from the Chief of Naval Operations.

Q: I guess it has!

PEDAGOGICAL CONSIDERATIONS

Mr. K.: Under the heading of pedagogical considerations, I would note that the military services, including the Navy, have in the recent past at least been in the forefront in experimentation with and adoption of new teaching techniques.

Q: You say "in the recent past." This wasn't always true,

was it?

Mr. K.: Well, I think that dating back to World War II the Navy has been in the forefront, but the Navy training organization, as we've noted previously, wasn't a very healthy organization up until that time. So we were probably following along up to that time, but at that time it became essential to get into the forefront.

Q: Just as a preface, this implies close cooperation with civilian exponents in this area, does it not?

Mr. K.: Yes. I think perhaps I've already mentioned that during World War II a large number of civilian educators came into the Navy in uniform and many of them elected to stay on. Many of them are even today exuding a considerable influence on the pedagogical outlook of the Navy.

Q: And I would include you in that category.

Mr. K.: Yes, I would be honored to be in that category! For example, Clark and Sloan in their book <u>Classrooms in the Military</u> comment on this in a conclusion paragraph as follows:

> "It seems that the urgency of maintaining an efficient and effective combat force has evolved educational procedures in the military for successful mass technological training needed in civilian life quite as urgently as in the mili-

tary."

Clark and Sloan devote a couple of pages to a description of the Navy's training-device center, now the Training Equipment Center at Orlando, Florida, which pioneered in the creation of synthetic training devices. They call it an "almost fantastic institution" devoted to the creation of devices to facilitate teaching. The Navy uses many hundreds of aids and devices, some simple, others complex, costing several millions of dollars each. This supports the thesis that hands-on training is best. In the absence of actual seagoing equipment, a synthetic device that performs on-shore like the real thing in a ship or an aircraft is the next best.

It is interesting to note, in passing, that the viewgraph, or overhead projector which throws images on a screen, of hastily made or sophisticated transparencies was actually invented by a Navy employee then attached to BuPers and more recently with the Training Equipment Center at Orlando. In his work with training aids he became acquainted with a light-lens arrangements manufactured in France. The French version was not suitable for viewgraph purposes, but our employee convinced an American manufacturer to make some alterations--

Q: Will you name him?

Mr. K.: His name is George Beckwith, who has just now this last June retired and is still living in Orlando,

Florida.

The result is that the Navy, all the military and the civilian academic world inherited one of the most prolificic instructional devices extant even today.

Of course, the Navy was early in the field of closed-circuit TV, one of the first units anywhere having been installed at the Naval Academy, and with various forms of teaching machines. The results to date from these innovations have not been profound. The medium works, but not necessarily better or cheaper than the old-fashioned teacher-taught classes. We're still trying to improve and find better methods for their use.

Q: What's your judgment of that?

Mr. K.: My judgment is that one of the difficulties, in teaching by television is that it requires a fairly sizeable staff to continually create the software, to produce the lessons. Once you've got the lessons developed, why, then, there isn't much of a job in putting them on the air and transmitting them from one place to another. It's much easier to get hardware oftentimes than it is to get people to do software.

So we have quite a few installations in the Navy, but we don't really have any good production studios in the sense of being able to produce the materials--the teaching materials--in a really good pedagogical method. Consequently, the Training Command has now taken steps to reduce the number of studios down to three, the first of which is being installed at the present time on the West Coast in San Diego. They are trying thereby to pool the resources of production-oriented type people so that the materials that will be produced in the future, hopefully, will be better than what we have produced in the past. Therefore, it should become a more useful instrument.

Q: Is there any limiting effect on the flexibility of the teaching vehicle through this?

Mr. K.: Yes, I think there is in the same way that there is in using films. The Navy was one of the first to use films and to use them in great quantities, and we still use them in great quantities. But the films have to be used with a good deal of judiciousness on the part of the instructor to select the right film, for one thing, and to be in a position to interpret the film, and not just show movies. His purpose is to do some instructing. It's a vehicle, therefore, that has to be used with a considerable amount of discretion.

In the case of teaching machines, one of the first teaching machines that I remember having any contact with was immediately after or even while World War II was still on. It was a machine that was used by the aviation contingent of the Navy to train people in aviation pursuits-- what's an airplane and what are its characteristics and so on? You pushed the button and you could see whether you had the right answer. If you got the right answer, why, the machine told you so. But one of the difficulties that became so apparent when I visited a museum in New York and saw these Navy machines in fairly large numbers sitting around, about 90 percent of them were out of commission. They didn't have somebody to keep them in repair. This is one of the difficulties with teaching machines. They not only require somebody expert to feed them, but they require some other experts to maintain them. Therefore, you have to make a choice between using this technique, making good use of it and paying whatever it costs you, or else you use the old-fashioned method that you know will work and you can afford.

So, these things are known, there are lots of them in the Navy, but we really haven't learned yet, anyway, how to make the best use out of them.

More recently computers have been used to manage or assist instruction. There is promise of reduced trainee time by these efforts, but they're costly for the initial and updated program efforts they require.

Q: How would they be used?

Mr. K.: Well, for example, we have carried on many experiments in the use of them, to assist the learning process. The Naval Academy has been a forerunner in this field of using computers. They had an IBM 1500, which, of course, was a machine made expressly for instructional purposes. It didn't have much in the way of capacity and therefore, had limited utilization in the long run, but it was something that could be learned on. The Academy today has a real forward-looking and outstanding program in which they have succeeded in putting on computers various questions and various items of knowledge. The student can sit at a table and talk to a computer through an outlet and he can have a computer respond to him and he can learn individually in that manner.

We have tried it in other areas, too. It was carried on in San Diego for a couple of years--an extensive experiment on the use of computers for teaching electronics. The result of that experiment was that we could show that you could teach by the interaction between a student and a programmed computer. You could teach as well as you could in a classroom, and perhaps you could even teach him a little faster, especially if you let him proceed at his own rate.

But the limitations on the experiment were such that we didn't have enough outlets, enough capacity in the computers, so that we could make it cost-effective.

There is at the present time an effort going on in connection with the University of Illinois to conduct an experiment by which the Navy will have some twenty different locations--outlets at several locations. They will be tied into a computer in Urbana. A student, therefore, will be able to talk to and get response from a computer at a considerable distance from his location and over a fairly wide scope of subject matter.

The other way in which computers have been used and are being used and which gives considerable promise of success is in what is called computer-managed instruction. This means, in very brief terms, that a student works out the problems and he fills in certain blanks. These papers are then fed into a computer which may be at a considerable distance from where he did his work. The computer then corrects the paper and responds back to tell the instructor and the student where the student is weak and where he needs some additional emphasis. This is something that has been carried on at Memphis over a series of years. They are now ready to expand on this system and go out and get the services of a larger computer and get it programmed, but right at the minute it's held up because of lack of funds.

Q: I would think that would be more promising than the first example you cite, the student learning directly from the computer. You read out the interplay of two personalities which seemed to me rather valuable.

Mr. K.: I think there is promise in that first one, that is teaching by computer. It's obviously an expensive proposition but the Academy's experience has been--has shown promise. The Navy has invested at Annapolis several million dollars and has had the services and assistance of the Department of Health, Education, and Welfare in producing programs for use on their computers. So I think it's a valuable tool provided you can find a way to afford the initial investment and the upkeep investment that has to go into it.

Q: I would think the student would have to be highly motivated to begin with.

Mr. K.: Yes, I think this is true. The Navy's experience, however, on this kind of thing is that in the main a student is motivated, and when he has a chance to work by himself and he knows that his own efforts are either going to produce or not produce, he usually climbs in there and does it. Obviously, you weed out some, but the matter of motivation has not been an obstacle in any of our experiences up to date.

Q: How does the state of this experimentation in the Navy stack up with what is being done in private universities and perhaps in the other services?

Mr. K.: Well, there has been a lot done in universities. Penn State, for example, has been one of the leading institutions, and I've already mentioned the University of Illinois. But I think that on the whole the Naval Academy, in my estimation and according to my information, ranks well in the forefront of any educational institution in the country. This is not to say that others haven't tried it, haven't done it. The Air Force, not in their Academy as far as I know, but in other instances has experimented, has tried things out, and is still trying things out. Of course we're watching over each other's shoulders and if anybody comes up with a breakthrough, why, we're all going to be there! We'll enjoy it together.

I think one of the most promising innovations in this field of educational learning techniques is what the Navy is calling self-paced individualized instruction.

Q: That's intriguing!

Mr. K.: The individual's success in these areas shows a possible saving of trainee time and instructor time on the order of 30 percent. This is not a new idea in educational circles. Many trial efforts have been made to allow students to proceed at their own learning pace. However, the Navy's procedure differs from most all other efforts in, first, making a task analysis of the job to be accomplished and then carefully programing the instruction materials to reach that objective in the least feasible time. But the Navy does not stop there. A student is offered a number of different instructional vehicles from which he can choose the one or more that suits his learning style best. The different vehicles range from written explanations to programed texts, visual and sound cassettes, to breadboard and hands-on laboratory equipment.

Much emphasis now is being given to getting forward with this innovation within the newly organized Training Command.

Q: Who does the task analysis?

Mr. K.: This is being done by a variety of organizations, I guess you might say. As we stand at the minute, there is a rather comprehensive effort that is being made by the personnel research organization under the Chief of Naval Personnel, which is called The Naval Operational Task Analysis Program (NOTAP). This is designed to explore a great many or all the jobs, you might say, that are being done by any specialty or any rating in the Navy.

They have concentrated their effort first on the aviation-type ratings and are now expanding into some of the other ratings. In the meantime the training organization looked upon this as being so worthwhile in the way of being able to reduce the learning time that several years ago we proceeded in the basic electronics field and set up a group in San Diego to do the analysis and to construct the course structure in such a way as to cut down on the learning time. We weren't content to do this with just one effort. There were actually three different efforts, one at San Diego, one at Great Lakes, and one at Treasure Island, all going on in somewhat different style at the same time. And when this experiment was completed our people chose what they thought was the best of the three, or a combination of the three, and put it into effect in the two places where the fundamentals of electronics are taught. These are San Deigo and Great Lakes.

We are now teaching by this methods, by this self-paced individualized instruction. This means that the individual chooses his vehicles for learning, with the guidance of an instructor. His learning is self-paced because he goes as fast as he can. Some people, because they've had the background, can finish up what used to be a six weeks' course in a matter of a few days. Others take longer. Some take longer than six weeks. But the average has now dropped from six weeks down to four weeks, and when you consider that the annual input is about 12,000 a year and you save two weeks on each of 12,000 people, you've made a substantial saving.

Q: But since they all complete the course at different times, you have some built-in headaches for assignments, don't you?

Mr. K.: You do as long as you don't have a course into which you can put the individual right immediately. Fortunately, most of our electronics courses begin each Monday, so that the maximum that you could have as a gap would be, perhaps, four days from the time that he gets through with one course and takes up the next one.

However, the answer to that in the long run is to get all of those courses self-paced and individualized also so that he picks up a new course the day after. He completes one he hasn't had to wait for anybody else. You can make mistakes, and we have made them, all right, in this area because you would naturally think, we'd better start programing the elementary course first. That's what we did in one instance and then we found just exactly what you detected here, that when you got the individual through he had to sit and wait for the rest of the people to catch up with him so that he could join up with them in the course that had not yet been programmed for self-pacing.

Now, if we were going to do it over again, what I would suggest we do is to program self-paced, individualized more-advanced courses first so that the individual coming along could start in one of those courses and go at his own speed. Then we could individualize the more elementary courses, and we'd have the whole thing solved. You don't always see these things right away.

I was present one day when the Army people--research people--were telling about their efforts in this connection and somebody asked the question, well, when you get this individual that completes that whole course in one day, what happens to him then? Doesn't he just have to sit and wait for the rest of the people to catch up with him? And the individual on the platform said, yes, unfortunately, that's the case today. But, he said, that's not a research problem, that's a detailing problem, therefore it's not ours!

Q: That's passing the buck, isn't it!

In permitting the student to select his favored method of procedure, have you noticed a pattern? Is there some method that's more favored than others?

Mr. K.: No, I don't believe so. I wouldn't want to leave the impression that the student is entirely on his own in this. There is an instructor who is present and available and who, therefore, is in a position to guide the student in the direction that appears to him to be most favorable. So the two of them get together on what's best for the student.

On the other hand, I think the average student is pretty apt to use all of the five or six different vehicles that are available to him. The difference being, however, that one of the methods, one of the vehicles available is a written text. So he can sit and read that text and if he finds, gee, I know all of this because I studied it somewhere else before, why, he's in a position to go on to the next lesson.

Then, the same material is also given to him visually and in sound so that he can look at it and he can listen to it at the same time. Therefore, he has the double chance, you might say, of taking it in by two different senses at the same time and proeeding faster than he might otherwise. This doesn't mean that he has exclusively used one method as opposed to anoher, but he has had the opportunity to select from these various ones and if he finds he doesn't gain anything by listening to it, he can discard that.

On the other hand, a very valid part of this effort is in casettes, where you have the sound and a picture at the same time, and obviously this is one of the best ways to learn.

Q: These being modern students, is there any evidence that the learning process is enhanced by listening rather than visual reading?

Mr. K.: I have no real statistics on that. I would guess, however, that the average student even today, yesterday, or any other day, finds it difficult to learn by just reading a passage and making it stick, you might say. He needs some reinforcement of some sort. Either the professor tells him again what he read in the book or questions enough so that he begins to collect things up together.

Q: But I was thinking with the modern generation, his experience has been largely through communication through television and what have you.

Mr. K.: Yes, and I think this is one of the values, one of the reasons why the cassette with a picture arrangement so that he can flip from one to another, and the picture is shown and the recorder talks to him at the same time is one of the better ways in which people learn. On the other hand, of course, as we educators learned long ago, you learn best by doing. Therefore, as I've indicated, you don't overlook the necessity of having the tools and the breadboards and the devices available so that he gets his hands in and has to do something as well as read about it or see it in a picture. This is one of the important things. When he gets through, whether he learns what he learns by reading or listening, the final test really comes in ascertaining if he can do what it is that he's supposed to have learned how to do? Not just can he give you the words back, but can he go through the process. Therefore, there has to be that laboratory aspect cranked in there and this, of course, I think to the modern youth is an important part of the learning process. He got in there himself and he did it. He didn't just see a demonstration of it, this was something he did on his own.

Q: Have you discovered any correlation between the retention of learning and the modern speed-up methods, you say saving 30 percent time?

Mr. K.: No, I don't know that there is a way. Of course, all learning is tested on the basis of examinations that they take. Anything that I know of or have been able to discover would indicate that the learning is just as secure, let's say, by this method if not better. The man gets there faster, he gets on the job quicker, he gets into the next phase quicker, and he likes that. Of course, in most instances, he's a willing candidate. I think the retention is bound to be good. That's an opinion rather than a proven fact.

Q: In the application of the new equipment and so forth,

did you get ready cooperation from the Congress and the appropriations committees?

Mr. K.: I think you would, if you got to Congress and you explained that you need say a million dollars for this kind of a thing or this machine, and it's going to do this, that, or the other thing. Congress would sit up and take notice and say that's fine, Sonny, here's your million dollars, go and do it. But you don't get to the Congress with that, and it's very uphill work.

Q: You mean you have to fight your own people?

Mr. K.: You've got to fight your own way through. The way in which budgets are built is if you want anything more or different than you had last year, why it stands out like a sore thumb and somebody along the way is bound to nick that off before it gets very far upstream, just because you asked for more, you see. This is the way budgets are built.

I recall, for example, one instance when we were working on this matter of getting further along than we had at that time and further along than we are not in teaching electronics and other ratings by this kind of method. It cost investment money, of course. It cost money in terms of people to construct the courses, to do the task analyses, to keep things going in that direction. It cost money for the cassettes. It cost maybe half a million dollars for the two places where we put the original courses in, after we had got the courses constructed and knew what we wanted to do--I mean just the hardware cost. So, you build a case.

You go to the Chief of Naval Operations and you say in a letter, look, we've had great success with this thing; we can show you that we can save 300 man years or 2,000 man years by 1975, and so on. If somebody will only loan us or let us have a million dollars for investment in 1973, why, we can do all of this by 1975. We'll show you how you can save $10 million a year. You put it down in black and white. Then you get back a letter that says, gee, that's fine; what you ought to do is go ahead and make some of those savings that you can foresee for the future so that you can use that for the investment, and then proceed, we're all in favor of it. But you can't have a million dollars.

So, how do you get there? Well, you scrimp and you scrape and you say, well, instead of painting that building or putting a new roof on that building this year, we're going to screen off a quarter of a million dollars and we're going to buy these things and we're going to do it. We're going to do it by pulling on our own bootstraps. That's the way to get it done.

Q: Does that reaction, when it comes consistently, act as a discouragement to your enthusiasm?

Mr. K.: Oh, I think so, yes. It certainly does to the people who are involved. I mean, they've got an idea, they're ready to go. I can tell you how discouraged they were as we went along on this thing. But, it's just the way the world is, that's all!

You're discouraged, yes, but you go and take a look at it and say, oh, well, the heck with it, we'll try again tomorrow. What else have we got to do? And you get there.

Q: Now, Sir, in the education of a man you have to be concerned about the whole man. You've been talking about methods of teaching. What about his concomitant social adjustment and growth keeping pace with his learning? What measures are taken there?

Mr. K.: Well, we haven't really found any need for anything different in this regard than has been the case in other instances. In the majority of cases, our elementary courses, class "A" schools, and so on, the individual has arrived from civilian life, he went through recruit training, he's typically a bright young fellow, he isn't married, he doesn't have any family ties yet, his business in life is going to school and then go on liberty. This is the way life is and this is the way he takes it in stride. And I don't believe the fact that you speed up his getting through school makes any real difference to him.

Q: I was thinking in an area which, of course, touches

on ordinary education certainly, and that is in the area of public speaking. What efforts are made to teach a man to express himself publicly, vocally or in writing?

Mr. K.: There are opportunities in this for him to express himself, usually, I would have to agree, to his instructor, either in response to oral quizzes or when he's in need of help and expresses himself as to what is his need and so on. It has the disadvantage, if you wish, from a social educational program of what you might call group therapy, or people getting together and chitchatting, and so on. But there are courses which the Navy provides in things like instructor training, leadership. I've mentioned the race relations aspects and drug abuse. These kinds of things are done, and still done, on the basis of learning as a group. In other words, trading back and forth and chitchatting back and forth. You perhaps can make a point, well, he lost something there, when he didn't have the chance to engage in back-and-forth chatter, but he has a chance all the time. He can talk. There's no limitation on his talking to his fellow students and comparing notes with them while he's in this process. In other words, he's not isolated completely from civilization during the process.

So, while you can say that in the old-fashioned method where the teacher asked questions and the student responded, and 10 percent of the students were the only ones who responded, 90 percent didn't get much out of it anyway. So that maybe we're losing something for that 10 percent, but he's the fellow that's gregarious enough so that he'll get there anyway.

Q: I take it there's no real overt kind of program for inducing self-expression?

Mr. K.: No, and there never has been really in the old-fashioned method. In other words, the Navy Technical school we're talking about here is a trade school type of thing anyway, in which you watch the instructor do something and then you try to emulate him. The only thing is that you were on a lockstep basis and you all did it on the same day on the same experiment and then you went on the next day. That's the only difference really.

We're giving the individual a series or a selection of means by which he can progress at his own rate.

It would be inappropriate to leave this discussion with reference to Navy training in a sense that it is largely reliant on classroom theory, training aids, and synthetic devices. A hallmark of Navy training is that which is conducted in the laboratories using models of the actual shipboard equipment. Some of this is in the form of relatively small black boxes containing electronic gadgets, others are large and occupy huge buildings specially built for the purpose, like the actual installation of a shipboard, 1,200-pound boiler plant now under construction at a cost of many millions at Great Lakes, Illinois.

Q: This is the Link trainer method, isn't it?

Mr. K.: Well, the Link trainer is a trainer, instead of the airplane itself. What I'm saying here is that what's going in at Great Lakes is actually the boiler, the same boiler that would go in a destroyer. Not a model of it and not a thing that acts like it, but it itself. This is, as I say, the hallmark of Navy training, that you use the real thing when you can.

Q: And that's sort of expensive, isn't it?

Mr. K.: Yes, it is expensive, but nevertheless it is best when it's feasible and so the Navy uses the actual hardware as the vehicle on which it trains its officers and enlisted personnel, when it can.

Q: Maybe sometimes it saves a real boiler!

Mr. K.: This is right. Obviously the reason I mentioned the 1,200-pound boiler right now is that this is one of the pieces of machinery that the Navy is having a real lively time with. We have planned this 1,200-pound-per-square-inch boiler installation for operator training. We have a 1,200 pound boiler at Philadelphia now, but it is used primarily to train people in advanced maintenance aspects of boilers. What we need is one that we can use primarily to teach them which valve to turn when on an operational kind of basis, and that's what we'll have at Great Lakes.

We have known of the need for this for at least ten years and we have tried real hard, through the military construction program over that period of time, to get the building into which to put the actual boiler so that you've got something to work on. Now, obviously, the difficulties they've had with the boiler technicians and with boilers themselves in recent episodes aboard ship have given impetus to the point where this has become one of the higher-priority items in the whole Navy effort--to get that boiler in there and to get it going as a part of the training program. But I think it illustrates also another point that I've made several times, and that is that you really have difficulty getting what you know you need until it becomes a crisis. Then, all of a sudden, you get help from all over everywhere. In the case of a boiler, it's taking about three years to actually get the building built and the boiler installed after you've got everything in shape so that it's going in the right diretion.

In 1975 and maybe by 1974 we'll have a plant out there that will be equal to none in the world, but it's hard work.

Q: There's one other area--aspecialized area--of training, were you involved in that, the preparation and training of men for service on Polaris submarines?

Mr. K.: Yes. The Bureau of Naval Personnel has been involved in putting people on the FBM submarines, Polaris, The A-1s and A-2s and A-3s, and now Poseidon. We're getting ready, of course, for Trident. All the way through the personnel planning aspects, the school aspects, getting the right numbers of students in the right school, the right number of instructors--qualified instructors--there at the right time, and so on and so forth has all been a Pers-C problem up to recently. Now the responsibility has shifted to the Chief of Naval Training.

Of course, we've had very vigorous help. I expect probably the Special Projects Office would put it the other way around--that we had assisted the Special Projects Office. But there has been a real close relationship between the people-training element and the people who are creating the hardware and making sure that the submarines are manned with well-trained personnel.

Q: Did the vigorous director of the whole program at first, Admiral Raborn, get involved in this area?

Mr. K.: Yes, we had real close relationships with Admiral Raborn, learned how to make PERT charts. We followed his program with him and were with his people continuously, and in more recent years with Admiral Levering Smith.

Q: Were there any special requirements for enlisted personnel serving in Polaris? I mean, did they have to have a higher aptitude?

Mr. K.: They were selected from the same group of people that nuclear-power people were, electronics technicians were, and so on—the upper 10 percent usually. You might have to dip down a little if you ran short sometimes, but those Polaris submarine people, or submarine people in general, are pretty apt to be from the high-quality people in the Navy.

Q: And since you are concerned about the many aspects of it, did this involve morale as well? Did you take that into consideration—the long, long days and weeks of service without any high points?

Mr. K.: The psychological aspect became a problem, but this was not a problem that you were able to visualize very well when the individual was going through training. In other words, you couldn't screen them out too well. As long as they got by the normal psychological examinations when you were selecting them in the first place. But I'm sure that the forces afloat ran into this in later years and it undoubtedly had a rather decisive effect, especially on the retention rates of nuclear-power people, which in recent years has become decidedly worse than what was visualized. This has meant the necessity of boosting up by great quantities the number of people going to school in nuclear power, which is related because the Polaris goes to sea in nuclear-powered submarines, so there's a relationship between the two.

Q: What about the psychological aspects as they pertain to the general training program?

Mr. K.: Well, you run into psychological difficulties, of course. We have many students, hopefully not inordinately large numbers, who flunk out of courses and flunk out on purpose because they don't like the course that they've gotten themselves into or some psychological effect has come into being that causes them to change their minds about liking it. This is the kind of thing that you foresee and try to take into account, and it hopefully comes in fairly predictable quantities. You can foresee that in one group in this kind of instruction, because of our experience, you'll have a large loss, or in this one you'll have insignificant losses. So your input takes that into consideration when you're estimating how many you're going to get out.

In some kinds of training the screening is made purposely pretty difficult to get through, and nuclear power is one of them, or has been, at least, until recently. I don't really know about it today, but until recently the attrition rate in people going into nuclear power who went into the machinists' mates school, went through various other training which included the fundamentals of nuclear power and then the nuclear reactor training and so on, losing some at each of these stops along the way amounted at one time to more than 60 percent. So, you do have attrition for various reasons, not necessarily the volition of the individual every time, but his inability to hack whatever standards you have set.

Q: A man told me one time about a very interesting method of screening down at Pensacola in the 1930s, I think it was—the use of gliders for a short period of time at the outset of the course, and the men who successfully maneuvered the gliders apparently were being qualified to go on. But a lot were eliminated right at that point. Is there anything else in the realm of training that might be comparable with that?

Mr. K.: I don't think of anything that would correspond with that one on gliders. Of course, we do obtain much of our attrition as far as aviation pilots are concerned these days in the preliminary training programs that are conducted in connection with the Naval Academy and the NROTC, where the Navy supports flight training of commercial type for selected students who volunteer. So if the individual then goes to a civilian flight school for his 35 hours of flight training and 35 hours, or whatever it is these days, of ground school, and he doesn't take to it, why, obviously he's not a suitable candidate to go to Pensacola for further flight training. We get quite a lot of attrition that way.

On the other hand, of course, flight training is one of the areas where you do get a high attrition rate.

Q: I wasn't thinking necessarily in terms of aviation.

Mr. K.: I realize that you weren't, but I don't really think of any. You usually find out in the first few weeks that the individual's in a school whether he's going to take it or not. And so most of your attrition takes place in the first half of the course.

Q: Industry employs aptitude tests rather heavily. Is this employed also in the Navy?

Mr. K.: The Navy has a series, batteries, of tests, and before the individual is allowed to subscribe for a school he goes through this battery which is the best device now known to ascertain whether the individual has the aptitude for it. Yes, it's an aptitude test, along with various other measurements. So, only those who reach a specific score are allowed to continue into or to choose that vocation.

Yes, the Navy along with the other military services is a very comprehensive testing institution. Everybody is tested before he goes very far.

Q: How do you keep abreast of all these developments?

Mr. K.: I don't, really. Not these days anyway. I used to be, in BuPers, in the middle of all these things so that rarely did anything go on that I wasn't--didn't have a foot in it somewhere. But more recently--and this is why I say every once in a while that this is the way it used to be--I'm not really that much up to date.

THE NROTC PROGRAM

The next area I was going into was NROTC. You mentioned your particular interest in that the other day when we were together. Is that agreeable?

Q: Yes. Glad to have you talk about it.

Mr. K.: The Army and the Navy have relied on ROTC units in civilian colleges for many years. The first Navy units were established in 1926 at the University of California at Berkeley--

Q: This was Admiral Nimitz' baby!

Mr. K.: Right--at the University of Washington, Yale, Harvard, Northwestern, and Georgia Tech. During World War II the Navy had numerous programs for the early selection and education of prospective naval officers, like the V-7 and the V-12 programs. The successful procurement of officers prompted the Navy to expand its NROTC program. However, the Navy introduced a new aspect, which has sometimes been called the Holloway Program, after Rear Admiral James L. Holloway, Jr., who headed the board designed to formulate, among other things, the Navy's officer-procurement plans. The new aspect was the subsidy for tuition and books and payment of $50 a month toward other expenses. The Congress authorized in 1946 payment of the scholarship expenses. In effect, the Holloway Plan provided for two types of NROTC students. One was called "regular," those who were selected in national competition and whose tuition and books were paid for fully plus $50 a month plus pay and expenses while engaged in three summer cruises. The other was called "contract," and the students were enrolled in a program after matriculation in the college of their choice. Contract students took the same naval science courses as were prescribed for regular students for a total of 24 semester hours. However, contract students received pay of $50 a month during only their last two academic years and pay and expenses during only one summer cruise.

Q: You couldn't be a contract student unless you were in a school where they had a unit?

Mr. K.: That's true. You could not be at that time.

The Navy undertook the selection of additional units. This was in 1946, considering the merits and willingness to cooperate of virtually all of the leading civilian universities in the country. This effort was headed primarily by Dr. Arthur S. "Beanie" Adams, who was a graduate of the Naval Academy recalled to active duty during World War II and later the President of the American Council on Education.

Forty-six units were added at that time on the basis of criteria developed largely by Dr. Adams.

Q: What were some of his requirements?

Mr. K.: One criterion was that, insofar as feasible, the

distribution of units geographically was to bear a close relationship to the numbers of high-school students being graduated at that time. Other criteria were the willingness to cooperate and the prestige of the institution in its own locality, and so on. The list of 46 included the Ivy League schools, but also included a number of prominent State-supported universities, such as the University of Wisconsin, the University of Missouri, andmany others.

The Navy stood alone as the only service authorized to subsidize NROTC students until 1964, when the Army and the Air Force also gained similar congressional authorization.

Q: Why was the Navy favored first?

Mr. K.: The Navy was the only one that really had a felt need, I think, at that time. There was no Air Force, of course, and the Army had been getting along with their ROTC programs for a long time. Theirs was really what amounted to the Navy's "contract" program, so they didn't feel the need for it up to that time. But they began to see in the early 1960s that the Navy was doing pretty well and they weren't doing so well.

The Congress has also raised the allowance for scholarship expenses from $50 up to $100 a month. The NROTC scholarship program, as it is now called rather than "regular" in the later legislation, has proven to be a very valuable source of real outstanding officers, many of whom have chosen to make the Navy a career.

For example, my records show that in 1969 nine flag officers, who were NROTC grads, were on active duty, three USN flag officers were on the retired list, and there were eight USNR flag officers on the rolls.

The initial congressional authorization permitted the Navy an enrollment of not more than 15,400 students at any one time, not more than 14,000 of whom could be fully subsidized. However, by executive agreement between Secretary Forrestal and President Truman the scholarship portion was limited to 7,000. The Navy never quite reached the 7,000 but came close a few times. In 1964 the Navy enrollment was running about 5,500, so Congress considered that to be a good ceiling for each of the services and so regulated by law. The ceiling has since been slightly lifted and now stands at 6,000 for the Navy, with some Navy aspirations evident in the face of the all-volunteer force to lift the ceiling to 10,000.

The Navy established a complex but comprehensive national selection system for scholarship students which gave weight by states to their number of high-school graduates. It included a written exam, interviews by state screening committees, and other hurdles, such as physical qualifications. It has been a popular program with approximately 20,000 new enrollments annually.

We try to be cost-effective in this program, as in others, so instead of giving each school the same quota we arranged about 1957 for the grouping of schools based as nearly as we could on the cost-effectiveness of the product produced.

At first, because of our limited experience with the retention of graduates, we had to allow tuition costs to be a big factor. Thus, a higher-tuition Ivy League school got a smaller quota than, for example, the University of Texas which charged less tuition. Later refinements considered such factors as student output and the retention experience together with the popularity of the school. This latter factor proved to be an essential one because there was nothing to be gained by granting a large quota to a college not popular enough to gain sufficient volunteers to fill the quota.

Adoption of the quota system brought forth a deluge of wrathful correspondence and other communications from most all of the Ivy League schools, who held we were discriminating against the private schools in favor of the state-supported schools. And I guess we were. We had great pressure through the Congress and the White House and the Secretary of Defense designed to convince us of the error of our ways. We held our ground.

A few years later it was our turn to complain when we discovered that some, one in particular, of the Ivy League schools were offering their own scholarships to NROTC candidates we had nominated to them, and then the candidate would turn down the Navy's offer. We suggested to these institutions that that was not really a fair way to play.

Q: Then he could be replaced by someone else?

Mr. K.: Yes. For example, some of the popular Ivy League schools could be given as many as 125 names, from which they could choose 25, which would be their quota. So if they picked out somebody off the list and gave him a scholarship, they could still pick their 25 Navy and they would then get the pick of the crop for their own scholarships.

Q: But what value to the student himself, the one who was supported by them, rather than by the Navy?

Mr. K.: It gave him a scholarship in an Ivy League school with no commitment to any military service.

Q: Would he get credit afterwards from the Navy?

Mr. K.: He disassociated himself from the Navy. He was now one of Harvard's boys, for example, and didn't have any interest in the Navy because he got something better. They'd offered him something better than the Navy could offer him or would offer him, so he didn't have any interest in joining the Navy any more after that.

In passing it should be noted that those institutions that complained most loudly about the Navy's quota system were the principal ones which elected to drive NROTC units from their campuses when student dissension reached its peak in the late 1960s.

Q: Did the institution have any real control over that?

Mr. K.: I don't know. In my estimation, they did, yes. The institution had control or should have exercised control over them. Let me put it this way, there were institutions that did exercise control over their faculties and over their dissenting student groups, and there were some who did not. Among the ones who did not were this group of Ivy League ones that complained most loudly before about the quota system.

Today we either have removed or will soon remove NROTC units from all New England Ivy League schools and from Stanford, Columbia, and Princeton. This is unfortunate but this is the way the academic fraternity insisted on playing. We had some real rough conversations with the school administrations at that time.

Q: Would you talk a little about some of those?

Mr. K.: Well, yes. We tried hard to convince the administration, for example, in these institutions that they should make the choice and not leave it to a part of their faculty. The usual dissenting portion of the faculty were members of the arts and sciences faculty and not all the others. Therefore, it wasn't fair, you might say, to their other schools for them to give in to the arts and sciences faculties. As I say, there were many negotiations and some of them at various times were rather fruitful. We have had some negotiations more recently about going back on the campus in some of these institutions. Brown, particularly, has set forth some indications of a desire to have the Navy come back. They have not, however, succeeded in getting themselves to the point where they're willing to come back on the Navy's terms, so we're not back in.

Q: Do you envision any change in this attitude now that the Vietnam War has come to an end?

Mr. K.: I don't think there'll be any difference just because the war has come to an end, but I think there is a feeling among many faculty people and the staffs of some of these institutions that they think now in retrospect that it was the wrong way to go and they would like to get an NROTC back. Of course, the Army and the Air Force have continued to stay in some of these institutions. They weren't willing to meet the Navy's terms, however, so we have withdrawn.

The going was rough in places like the University of Pennsylvania, Michigan, Minnesota, Colorado, and a few others, but painstaking negotiations and the intestinal fortitude of their academic leaders has resulted in the Navy remaining in these institutions. So I'm saying that there were some that resisted the internal pressures to the extent of negotiating on a favorable basis.

Q: You spoke about some of the Eastern universities not

being willing to meet the Navy's terms. What are the bones of contention in this area?

Mr. K.: Well, the two conditions that the Navy has insisted on are really conditions which we interpret as being prescribed by law. One of those is that the professor of naval science must be recognized by the institution as a member of the faculty, and secondly that the institution must agree to give some college degree credit for naval science courses. The law makes these two clear, but I admit that they're subject to interpretation on the latter point because it says that the institution shall be agreeable to providing the course of instruction which is prescribed by the Secretary of the Navy. We have interpreted that to mean that this requires the institution to give some credit toward a degree, not insisting on the 24 credits that we negotiated back in 1946, but on some credit for naval science courses.

So those were the two conditions. The initial formula was designed to ensure the school would grant 24 semester hours for naval science courses. This has been compromised over the years as the institutions, aided and abetted, in some cases, by accrediting agencies, such as in the engineering specialty, have reduced the amount of credit. However, the Navy still insists on being granted some academic credit toward a degree.

It may be interesting to note in passing that whereas

in the past more credit difficulties were experienced in the engineering schools, the more recent eruptions occurred usually in the liberal arts department of the institutions involved. These more recent outbursts of campus dissension were not the first such difficulties experienced by the ROTC, although they had the most far reaching results. Student elements at institutions like the University of Wisconsin and Cal, Berkeley, had registered protests against military units on their campuses in prior years. At one time serious consideration was given to withdrawing from the Berkeley campus, but the Navy persevered and we're still there. At the moment things are quiet.

Q: It seems to me that in the case of some institutions the whole problem was a great deal broader than just the Navy unit on the campus. I mean it got to the point where there was opposition to all government contacts and contracts and so on, the whole spectrum.

Mr. K.: Yes, there's no question about that. It was a broader effect and the school administrations had real difficulties on their hands. On the other hand, I suspect that the schools like Harvard, for example, succeeded in overcoming opposition to their accepting whatever it amounts to these days, but say about $100 million dollars' worth of research contracts from the federal government. But they didn't succeed in retaining the Navy ROTC, which is too bad because it was one of the initial institutions--one of the initial cooperating institutions as far back as 1946.

In recent years there's been a trend in the direction of new units in predominantly black universities and toward militarily oriented schools, such as the Citadel and the Maine Maritime Academy.

Q: This is a new development?

Mr. K.: This is a recent development. From 1946 until late 1960 there were 52 units. These were the original units. There had been one added, that was MIT, but it had a contract student population only, no scholarships. There was and is a special kind of two-year, engineering-emphasis type of curriculum there.

But in recent years with the trend in the direction of the all-volunteer force and in the direction of race relations and so on, we have been going into the southern schools. We now have units also, in addition to the Citadel and the Maine Maritime Academy, in Prairie State, Texas, Savannah State, South Carolina, Southern University and A & M College in Louisiana, Jacksonville University, the University of Florida at Gainsville, Florida A & M in Tallahassee, and North Carolina Central at Durham, North Carolina. Not all of these are black schools, but once you start getting into that territory you gain a considerable amount of political pressure in the direction of accepting some others also. This is why there seems to be a multitude coming in.

Q: Is there any noticeable difference in the quality of the students enrolling?

Mr. K.: Not that one can see just yet. In some of them, like Prairie State, which has been in being longer than the others, we have had difficulty in getting volunteers, volunteers who could qualify for the program. Therefore, it remains a real small unit, and most of the others, so far, are small units because they have just recently started. It's really too early to answer that question.

Q: Will the Navy make any effort to get back into the other schools that have broken away from the program?

Mr. K.: The way things stand now, the Navy policy and position is to be receptive, to be ready and eager to discuss getting back into those schools, but it doesn't intend at the moment to take the initiative in that direction.

Q: Sort of watching and waiting?

Mr. K.: Watching and waiting, you might say, yes.

Q: You said a little earlier that the Navy thinks in terms of getting the Congress to increase, to raise, the ceiling for enrollees in the program. This implies that it would be possible to get these additional students?

Mr. K.: Yes, we think it would be. You see, you have candidates still eager to enroll, even though the draft has been cooling off. The number of candidates this past year I think was on the order of 22,000. Dividing 10,000 by three, you could assume you were going to have an input on an annual basis of about 3,000 a year. So you would still be able to select 3,000 out of 22,000 applicants. At this stage in the game we don't look upon the proposed increase in numbers as being a hazard in getting the ceiling raised.

It's a good program, good in the sense that it pays liberally. It pays $100 a month, it pays for summer duty, cruising, and it pays all college expenses, that is, for books and tuition and fees, and it's a chance for the individual who can't get that on his own to have a way of getting through college.

My subject of NROTC wouldn't be complete without mention of the Stearns-Eisenhower Board. This board which often was referred to as the Eisenhower-Stearns Board, after General Eisenhower became president of the United States, was called the Service Academy Board. In reality, Dr. Robert L. Stearns, then the President of the University of Colorado, was the chairman of the board and Dwight D. Eisenhower was the vice chairman. The board reported in January 1950.

The purpose of the board was essentially one of determining the future of officer-candidate education in the armed services. It was designed to settle the questions with respect to service academies, should there be one for all, one on each coast, maintain the status quo, or abandon military academies in favor of such sources as the NROTC? The recommendations of the board had two salient results. One, it retained the two academies then in being and added the Air Force Academy at Colorado Springs. Secondly, it retained the ROTC, separate in the three services, as a necessary and viable source of service officers.

Q: So it bought both programs?

Mr. K.: It bought both programs and we obtained the gospel on which we could support this concept.

Another point worthy of mention is the Navy Junior ROTC, which supports units in secondary schools for the purpose of indoctrinating students therein in the elements of military traditions and purposes, thereby actively promoting good citizenship. The Army had had units in high schools for many years. In view of the dissension among young groups then arising, certain congressional leaders, among whom Congressman F. Edward Hebert of Louisiana, now the Chairman of the House Armed Services Committee, was most vigorous. Considered that Junior ROTCs in secondary schools would be a valuable off-setting influence.

Q: And when was this?

Mr. K.: This was in the early-1960 era. Accordingly, a portion of the ROTC revitalization Act of 1964, which I have previously mentioned when the Army and the Air Force got into the ROTC Scholarship program contained provision for Junior ROTC units in all the services. The Navy was reluctant to engage extensively in this program because predicted expenditures seemed unwarranted by the anticipated benefit to the Navy that could then be foreseen. However, fortunately, you might say in retrospect, the Congress persevered and Junior ROTCs became mandatory in all the services.

Q: Was the Congress more generous with funds as a result of this?

Mr. K.: I would put it this way. To my knowledge, every time the Navy has gotten up there with an item in it for the Junior ROTC the Congress has said, "Hurray, you've got your money." In other words, resistance is not at the congressional level.

Q: It's one of their favorite projects!

Mr. K.: Yes. You know, you're always under a ceiling and so your problem is how much can I cram in under that ceiling for this program that I know will sell.

The number of units assigned to the Navy and Marine Corps was 275 out of a total of 1,200 prescribed by law for all the services. The Navy now has 175 active units with some in all states, except New York, where state law prohibits them. It will increase next year, probably up to 223 units.

Q: Is this the maximum it has had?

Mr. K.: This will be the maximum that we are entitled to at the present time because the Marines have the rest of the 275. Both the Marines and the Navy now would like to have some more.

Q: This bespeaks its success?

Mr. K.: Yes, I think so. Experience with this program has been gratifying. It's proven to be popular with the school administrators, even though the local schools are required to pay a fourth of the salary of Navy retired personnel who serve as instructors and administrators and who receive not less than what they would receive on active duty.

Its popularity is perhaps one of the best measures of the social impact of the program. In addition, early results from units in being indicate that approximately 25 percent of the high-school students who elect to participate are motivated to enter one of the military services. Accordingly, there is present evidence that the Junior ROTC may be a viable force in meeting the new conditions in the all-volunteer force.

Q: On the average, how many students are there in a given unit?

Mr. K.: We must have 100 minimum to have a unit. I suspect that the Navy must average about 150 per unit.

It has now been opened to female students. The Navy

is now hoping for a change in the legislation which will increase the 1,200 ceiling of total units for all the services so that the Navy can increase its participation up to perhaps 500 units.

Q: You don't see any difficulty in increasing the ceiling?

Mr. K.: Well, as I told a Marine friend the other day when we discussed this on the phone, all we've got to do is get the word to Chairman Hebert and he would put it in a bill without any more contention, but the paper work has to go through OSD and the Office of Management and Budget.

Q: What is the status of the naval instructor in the high school?

Mr. K.: He's a member of the faculty, and he gets his retirement pay, and the Navy pays one-half of the difference between his retirement pay and full active-duty pay, and the school pays the other half. There is at least one officer in each unit and the number of enlisted men is in accordance with how many students there are in the unit. So it's a cooperative enterprise in which the school has to contribute something and therefore has to want it badly enough to pay a little something for it. The Navy furnishes the uniforms and books and the curriculum and so on.

Q: Has the existence of a unit in a given school made any difference in the over-all attitude of the student body?

Mr. K.: We can only rely on the impressions that you get from the school administrators themselves, and the fact that they're anxious to have these units and they don't want to give them up. I would say, yes, they see a difference.

Q: Is it fair for me to deduce from your attitude that perhaps there's more enthusiasm for the junior units than there is for the senior?

Mr. K.: No, I don't think so. I think they're two different things, two different birds, so it would be unreasonable or difficult to compare them. I think there's enthusiasm on most of the campuses where we have senior ROTCs now, where they're still left, as far as that goes. We have great relationships with people at places like Purdue, for example, at the University of Southern California, the University of California at Los Angeles. They're great institutions and they think the Navy's a great institution also. We pat each other on the back, you might say.

Q: Is New York State the only state that prohibits?

Mr. K.: The only state that prohibits junior ROTCs in secondary schools.

Q: But on what basis?

Mr. K.: It's been the law ever since we started in this

business and I don't know how long before that--they don't want the military influence to get into their secondary schools, public schools. Some of the initial units we put into what's called the Navy honor schools because we had a relationship with those schools. We had units there already, so we changed the name of them, you might say, in those instances.

Q: In institutions of higher learning like the Citadel it would seem to be a very natural thing to have a unit?

Mr. K.: Well, they've had Army there for a long time, of course. The Citadel has given the Army part of its officers, I guess, ever since the Citadel was established. We had no real enthusiasm in the Navy for getting into a military school and competing, if you wish, against Army, which was already there. However, the Marines had begun to feel a crimp insofar as their sources of officer input were concerned. Since we furnished the Marines some 15 percent of the output or thereabouts of NROTC graduates they were part of the family. They thought they could do well at a place like the Citadel, so we went along with them and established a Navy unit down there on the premise that the Marines would get most of the benefit of it. As it turned out, I don't know what the true percentage is, but now probably about 80 percent of the students are Navy-oriented and the other 20 percent are Marine-oriented.

We went into Texas A & M at the instigation primarily

of the Marines who thought this was a good Marine potential. I'm not sure how this is working out. It's too new so far to get any statistics on it. But these are some of the influences, which operate on the basis of a corollary to Pascal's principle: one moves in a direction away from the pressure.

Interview No. 4 with Mr. Prent Kenyon

Place: Ballston Towers No. 2, Arlington, Virginia

Date: Thursday afternoon, 1 March 1973

Subject: Biography

By: John T. Mason, Jr.

Q: It's mighty nice to see you today. You're looking pretty chipper. I see you've gotten rid of your cold.

CAST OF CHARACTERS

Mr. K.: It's nice to see you, too, Jack. As I'm getting to the conclusion of my dissertation on Navy training I thought it might be interesting to talk about some of the high-level people that it has been my privilege to work with and to know in the past thirty years.

Up to this time I've mentioned a number of high-ranking naval officers and a couple of Navy or Defense secretaries who exerted more than passing influence on Navy education and training. I'm sure there were many others whose role did not fit neatly into my abbreviated statement of Navy training and its organization.

As I have mentioned, BuPers training most often proceeded under its own power and guidance without much attention from on high. Once in a while, though, as we have noted, training got a boost or at least some attention from the Navy leaders.

Q: And sometimes a monkey wrench was thrown into things!

Mr. K.: Right. I have noted parts played by Admirals Ernest J. King, Chester W. Nimitz, Jerauld Wright, Arthur Radford, George Anderson, James L. Holloway, Jr., Claude V. Ricketts, Bernard A. Clarey, and Elmo R. Zumwalt, Jr. This list reads almost like a "Who's Who" in Navy leadership over the past thirty years. There were others, some of whom we have previously mentioned. They include Admiral Arleigh A. Burke, of 31-knot fame, who established the Burke Scholarship Program while he was CNO. This program took highly qualified Naval Academy graduates and, after a year at sea, enrolled them in college courses of graduate study up to and including a doctorate.

This program has been modified many times since, but still exists. When Admiral Burke was CruDesLant, he wanted to reorient his afloat school at Newport to an activity ashore, and so recommended to CNO via BuPers. This occurred in one of the numerous times when resources were scarce and so BuPers couldn't see a way of supporting it. So the CNO was presuaded to turn down the CurDesLant's recommendation. CNO disapproval was signed by Arleigh Burke, who had arrived in Washington in time to say no to the recommendation he had made as ComCruDesLant!

Q: May I interrupt and ask you if you had anything to do with the suggestion he made at one time that there should be a summer course at the Naval War College for the teaching of writing and self-expression in that way. Selected naval officers would go up there for a short course?

Mr. K.: No. I didn't have anything to do with that particular suggestion. However, there have been courses in the summer put in at the Naval War College, in management, especially, for high-ranking naval officers. So this may have been aided and abetted some by Admiral Burke's desire to bring about better communications or better management on the part of high-ranking officers.

Later on we in BuPers helped Rear Admiral Charles E. Weakley, who was an old friend from the ASW days in the 1940s, to form a destroyer school at Newport, even to writing the first curriculum for it and, of course, finding the military billets and furnishing support. The school is now one of the Navy's best, located in a new building called Weakley Hall, which BuPers sponsored through the Congress.

Q: Has it changed materially from the original days?

Mr. K.: The destroyer school? No. It teaches just about the same courses as it did back in those days. There have been some added on, however. There is now about to be added on a course called a Surface Line Officers Course, which will broaden out the concept in such a way that officers from other type commands, such as amphibious and mine warfare and so on, in addition to destroyer people, would get some courses at the destroyer school.

Q: What does the basic curriculum comprise?

Mr. K.: It teaches officers how to be department heads on destroyers, primarily. It gives them all of the background, the seamanship aspects, the navigational aspects, and the engineering aspects that a skipper or a department head primarily in a destroyer would have to have in order to take charge of a department.

Q: Is this something that you personally helped to develop?

Mr. K.: I was in on primarily the matter of logistics, finding the resources and getting the school established. We had people who were professionals at curriculum-writing who actually put the meat on the bones as far as what was taught was concerned.

I mentioned also Secretary of the Navy James Forrestal, later the first Secretary of Defense, and Under Secretary Robert Baldwin, who exerted influence on Navy training in my tenure. Then there was Secretary Thomas Gates, also later Secretary of Defense, who while he was Secretary of the Navy fostered, supported, and virtually forced acceptance of what became the Naval Enlisted Scientific Education Program, which has been covered earlier in some detail.

Q: Is it your intention to dwell on some of these gentlemen at a little more length?

Mr. K.: No. I'm really getting toward the point where I would pick out a few to dwell on. I've got so many that I'm only concentrating on a relatively few.

Quotes from Admiral Alfred M. Pride and H. P. Smith--the latter in his capacity as CinCLantFlt--have been noted. Admiral Smith had previously served as the Chief of the Bureau of Naval Personnel. He at first experienced difficulty in appreciating the advantages of higher naval education, since he had risen to the heights without benefit thereof. However, after about a year as the Chief of Naval Personnel he became a staunch apostle of Navy training.

A quote from Admiral Radford in the Minutes of the Secretary's Advisory Board of Educational Requirements in 1961 will show the emphasis he thought training deserved:

"We wouldn't let the improved equipment go on the airplane until we had people that could take care of it. If that airplane got out to the front line with nobody understanding the equipment, it was no good. Even if you have money to buy them, it's not good to have a ship with equipment that is out of commission replacing an older type that will work."

I've often kidded my Naval Academy graduate colleagues about their penchant for making snap decisions. It seems to me that the Academy does a fine job, among other fine jobs, of teaching naval officers to make decisions in a hurry. This is understandable because a captain on the bridge often needs to make a hurried decision on course and speed, when to fire and when not to fire. This commendable trait for performance on the bridge sometimes, in my opinion, carries over into administrative matters where consideration of the alternatives might be wiser than snap judgments.

Q: Then you imply that the alternatives are not taken into consideration?

Mr. K.: Not many times. Therefore, you try to persuade that the alternatives ought to be looked at. My point here can be illustrated by an anecdote, a true one, that occurred relatively early in my naval career.

Captain Jimmy Holloway in 1945 was then in the billet that later became Pers C in BuPers. He served as an excellent front man in contacts with the outside world, arranging for the transfer of flag officers he didn't think were doing a good job and so forth. He paid little attention to the day-to-day business of the education and training world. He left that minutia to his division directors. That was the way we thought it should be. He took care of the big things, we took care of the little things.

Late one afternoon, as we members of the functional training section were assembling to join our ride pool in our office about three-quarters of the way down the long corridor of the seventh wing of the Navy Annex, there came this booming voice from the head of the corridor saying,

"Merrick." Lieutenant Commander Merrick was our leader and he rushed up the hall to meet Captain Holloway. When they were close together Captain Holloway said, "Merrick, do you have a harbor defense school on Fisher's Island?"

To which Merrick replied, "Yes, sir." Whereupon Captain Holloway said, "Well, close the son of a bitch."

Under the circumstances, Merrick, who was a smart young NROTC graduate, gave him the correct answer when he said; "Aye, aye, Sir."

It would be unfair to leave the story at this point. The school in question was one of mine, so I went home and scribbled well into the night setting forth the reasons why that school should not be closed just yet.

Q: So you disagreed with the decision?

Mr. K.: Yes, I disagreed with the decision. The war in the Pacific was still going strong. We had already considered with ComInch the closing of that school and had gotten a policy decision, albeit a lukewarm one, that settled it.

We wrote a paper--point paper these days--to Captain Holloway which Commander Merrick took to him early next morning. After listening to our side of the story, Captain Holloway immediately dictated a memo to Rear Admiral Randall Jacobs, then the Chief of Naval Personnel, which ended up to the effect "in view of the above, unless directed otherwise, I do not intend to close the harbor defense school."

Q: What was his animosity toward it in the beginning?

Mr. K.: He didn't really have any animosity, but the point is that he hadn't taken time to explore it at all. He had received a call from Admiral Jacobs, who in turn had received a class from Admiral Kelly, who was the Commandant of the Third Naval District, who had received a call from the people that wanted their club house back on Fisher's Island. Now that the war in the Atlantic was over, they were ready and willing to go back and enjoy the sunshine at their club house, and that was the place which we were using for the school.

Admiral Kelly was obviously under pressure, and he put Admiral Jacobs under pressure, who put Captain Holloway under pressure! But the pressure was resisted and we didn't close the school.

I have many fond memories of my association with Admiral Jimmy Holloway before, during, and after the time he was Chief of Naval Personnel. He was the one who taught me that when all else fails in solving a problem you employ your "administrative instinct." That was the way he solved many of his problems. I also learned from him to regard the Naval Academy as a sacred institution. This lesson was learned the hard way when I had the audacity to employ a mathematical ratio as a basis for reducing the military allowance of the Academy. Admiral Holloway's reaction to this maneuver was such as to convince me forever that some problems are not solved mathematically. But he was a fine scholar and gentleman whose impact on Navy education and training was monumental.

Q: In connection with him, do you want to give me a definition of his point of view of "administrative instinct"?

Mr. K.: His tendency was to consider those things which you were bringing up and look at the alternatives, but quite often he would then end the session by saying, "Well, my administrative instinct leads me to decide that this is the way to go."

Q: I found him of a philosophical turn of mind. Did you?

Mr. K.: Yes, oh, yes, very much so, and a very good naval officer, of course, as is indicated by his career. As we've said already, he was the sponsor of the Holloway Plan, which is still with us. He was the advisor to the Stearns-Eisenhower group as to what was the proper way to go so far as education in the military was concerned. So he had a real outstanding career in the education and training business, you might say.

Q: Did he, in your opinion, have all of the qualifications to be superintendent of the Naval Academy? What is the ideal?

Mr. K.: I think this is rather difficult to put your finger

on. In my experience there have been many different attributes of those who have occupied the chair--people who have occupied the chair at the Naval Academy. It would be difficult for me to say. I can answer your first question, though, without any difficulty. I would say yes, he was one of the ones that had the attributes to be a real outstanding superintendent of the Academy. All the people that have been superintendents have not necessarily come from the educational fraternity. Some of them have come into the educational fraternity after they were superintendent, but I don't think this is necessarily a compelling prerogative insofar as the superintendency is concerned.

The superintendent needs to be a good outstanding naval officer who upholds the principles of the naval service.

Another fast friend, colleague, and mentor was Rear Admiral Howard "Red" Yeager, whose tragic and untimely death occurred a few years ago in a fire at the commandant's quarters at Great Lakes as he endeavored to rescue his invalid wife, Jean. Admiral Yeager was an outgoing public relations type who knew everyone and they knew him in and out of the Navy. He was the type that succeeded in getting extra tickets to the Army and Navy game for congressmen when tickets were as hard to get as they are now for the Redskins' games.

His philosophy of operations was different from that of Admiral Holloway, although they were firm friends and

I'm sure that Red Yeager influenced many decisions Admiral Holloway made. When Admiral Yeager came into Pers C he called us all in and said, in effect, I don't know anything about training, so you fellows tell me what we should do and we'll do it. So we did, and he did. It was a prosperous era for education and training and we had relatively good success all up the line, but particularly in the Congress, since Admiral Yeager and Congressman Harry Sheppard, a Californian and Chairman of the Appropriations Subcommittee, were real good friends.

Among the accomplishments of the period was the initiation of the Naval Enlisted Scientific Education Program. The support that Admiral Yeager obtained from the Congress for Navy education and training is illustrated by the following quote from the House Report, 1957, DOD Appropriations Bill:

> "Many in the Navy Department have discussed extensively the difficulties experienced in securing and maintaining the skilled technicians required for the modern, present-day Navy. In this connection, the Chief of Naval Personnel has promulgated a program to train a certain number of enlisted personnel in civilian and advanced service schools so as to provide them with the broad background in particular skills needed by the Navy in this period of marked technical progress and advance. The order defining this program, as

set forth by the Chief of Naval Personnel, will be found on page 144 of the Committee Hearings Related to Amendments to the Budget for 1957."

"Navy personnel taking advantage of this program would be required to serve two additional years on active duty in the Navy for each year spent in civilian or advanced service schools, such additional service to begin after their first re-enlistment and after the completion of the special training course. Thus, the Navy is ensured a minimum return of two years of active service in the fleet for each year spent in training. The Navy Department and the Chief of Naval Personnel are to be congratulated on the forward-looking approach serving to importantly support the over-all solution of this difficult problem."

The Committee went on in another section of the report to suggest that the Secretary of Defense ought to have the other services, specially the Air Force, adopt this same kind of a program. It, in that area, stated, "The Navy program appears sound and should within the next few years do much to alleviate this major and very serious problem. Accordingly, the Committee strongly urges the Secretary of Defense to have a program along the lines of the Navy program developed for each of the other services."

Q: How popular was this recommendation with the other services?

Mr. K.: The other services have looked upon our program with a good deal of envy. Whereas the Air Force has a program that is somewhat similar, none of the other services up to this time has adopted the same premise as the Navy for enlisted men.

Q: Envy, but not emulation?

Mr. K.: Right. They have not emulated so far. Maybe they have greater success in getting technicians or getting them to stay, but the NESEP Program has proven to be a very valuable asset in getting technically qualified officers into the Navy. It started out, of course, as I expect we've said before, as an enlisted program, but it soon became one which developed commissioned officers.

Q: Do you intend to say anything more about Randall Jacobs? Did you have anything to do with him? I'm particularly interested in getting some data on him.

Mr. K.: He was the Chief of Naval Personnel soon after I came there. Therefore, I knew him, and also knew him rather distantly when he was Commandant of the Thirteenth Naval District, from which he retired. I didn't intend to say anything more here because his influence on the educational training, at least with my purview, was limited.

Q: I think of him in connection with the WAVES in particular. Are you going to talk about the WAVES and their

NOTE: Page 189 follows immediately. Number 188 was omitted by accident in the original pagination.

training program and education.

Mr. K.: No, I don't plan to.

Q: Could you? Would you?

Mr. K.: Yes. We, of course, have always had, in my tours anyway, women in our schools and have had programs for women and recruit training for women. I previously mentioned the fact that we had woman boot training at Bainbridge and that this was just recently moved down to Orlando, Florida.

There has been a good deal of emphasis given just within the last few months to having additional women come into the Navy, so the training organization has been taking steps to create additional facilities at Orlando so as to permit the Navy to more than double the intake of enlisted women. The Class A schools have been expanded insofar as quotas for women are concerned, so that every rating in the Navy for which there is a school today is now available. We don't have women in all of them yet, but at least the door is open. If they can qualify otherwise they're admitted into the schools in every rating that the Navy has.

Q: I was thinking of the early days in World War II when the WAVES, as a group, came into being, their future and their destination was largely under the control of the Bureau of Personnel, wasn't it?

Mr. K.: Yes, they were recognized at that time--at least this was my understanding--as being a valuable asset to the Navy. I know that there have been various times when consideration was given to abandoning the WAVES. They have at times been looked upon as a voluntary auxiliary which, therefore, could be abandoned at will. There have been suggestions along the way that the Navy could get along without its women officers and enlisted personnel. But it's obvious from recent developments that they have been extremely useful, and I expect as time goes on they're going to play a bigger part, actually.

Q: Yes, and they aim to be a permanent part. But in the beginning they looked upon themselves as something much more than an auxiliary service.

Mr. K.: Yes. Their leaders were then, as now, real talented women. From my acquaintanceship, anyway, I have always contended that there was a very vital need and use for women in the services.

Q: Do you have knowledge of the early days when apparently the Navy, as a whole, expected only a few women to be incorporated into the service, but the Bureau of Aeronautics had different ideas and came forward with highly developed plans which involved thousands of women rather than hundreds? Do you have any knowledge of that?

Mr. K.: No. I must have missed that somewhere along the

line. I think that in the early days there were quotas set by the Navy as to how many women could be gainfully used in the shore establishment. These quotas have stayed with us over the years with the number of enlisted women being about 5,000 and with about 10 percent as many officers, in other words, about 500 officers. This has been the steady contingent of women in the Navy all through the years until very recently when stops have been taken out and they're about to gain.

No, I don't know about that Bureau of Aeronautics episode.

To continue on with the discussion of Admiral Yeager. Admiral Yeager was good for our morale and we made many advances. One of his more important contributions was public relations. Admiral Yeager liked to make speeches, provided someone would write them for him. He knew the pub info people, so he went about the country advertising our wares, the Navy's education and training programs. They were enthusiastically received, and I think the understanding between BuPers and the fleets and the Reserves and the general public was much improved.

I recall being in Norfolk, Newport, and Atlanta, Georgia, with Admiral Yeager for these sessions. I was the slide turner for the viewgraph tranparencies we used which were relatively new then.

Q: What period of time was this?

Mr. K.: This was about 1956 or thereabouts. I was also with him in a presentation to a public relations and Reserve seminar in Oakland, California, which included some of the nation's leading movie producers. We appeared at the national convention of the American Legion in Los Angeles on the Sunday before Labor Day one year. Red Yeager's fame spread far beyond the Navy. Wherever we went the Cadillac dealer in that city was sure to call him to arrange a golfing date or other affair. I recall in San Francisco we were staying at the St. Francis Hotel on Union Square. Incidentally, the manager of the St. Francis was one of Admiral Yeager's very close pals.

Q: That's how you got in, I guess! They're always filled.

Mr. K.: Perhaps so. One morning as I stopped by the Admiral's room to pick him up on the way to his next speech I heard him say on the telephone, "Say, how about sending me something different than that purple one you sent me last night?" Accordingly, very soon a chauffeur-driven, all-white, shiny new Cadillac drew up in the front of the St. Francis and took us to the speech-making session and transported us during our stay in San Francisco.

Q: Incidentally, what was the connection with Cadillac dealers?

Mr. K.: I tried to learn from Admiral Yeager why the Cadillac people were so good to him. His story, and I have no reason to doubt it, was that the Cadillac people were planning to persuade him to come to work for them. They offered him a good salary but he continued to love the Navy so much that he resisted all outside offers.

It occurred to me that perhaps the fact that a Naval Academy graduate at about that time was the president of General Motors may have played some part in Cadillac's friendship.

This discourse needs to end, unfortunately, on a sad note. The last time I visited with Admiral Yeager was at Great Lakes when he was the Commandant of the Ninth Naval District. He had come there from duty as commander, Amphibious Command, Pacific Fleet. It was a few weeks before his death. He was all aglow with enthusiasm and anticipation, looking forward to retirement. He had purchased a new car especially configured so that Mrs. Yeager would be able to get in and out of it. The make of the car? Cadillac, of course!

My discourse on the cast of characters would not be complete without mentioning Vice Admiral Hyman Rickover.

Q: No, indeed!

Mr. K.: My acquaintanceship with him has not been close and, at times, not real pleasant. But he deserves mention as one who has had an influence on Navy education and training. This influence has not always been regarded in all quarters as constructive. For example, his criticisms of the Naval Academy program have often reached the public press and the ears of the Congress.

About 1960 I was assigned the task of writing a paper in defense of the Naval Academy. The paper was designed to show that, despite Admiral Rickover's attack, the Academy had fulfilled its mission well. As far as I know, the paper was never made public, so Admiral Rickover was able to persevere in peace, not knowing that anyone had endeavored to challenge his allegations.

Q: Who commissioned you to do this?

Mr. K.: This was at the time that Admiral Page Smith was Chief of Naval Personnel and he was anxious to have some ammunition to be able to refute the accusations that Admiral Rickover was sending forth.

Q: Why was Rickover qualified to speak in terms of educational systems?

Mr. K.: I don't know whether he had any particular qualifications, but a successful man quite often takes the position that he is well qualified to talk on any subject! And you can be assured that Admiral Rickover in his field is a real success. That would be about as good an answer as I could give you on that.

Anyway, he has proclaimed, as you know, against the program of the Naval Academy--it's been too soft and not sufficiently intellectual, and all of these other kinds of accusations. I would presume that someone with a head wiser than mine decided not to tangle with Admiral Rickover. Such an entanglement would be dangerous! Admiral Zumwalt tells the story about the time Vice Admiral William R. Smedberg III, then the Chief of Naval Personnel, and Vice Admiral Rickover were feuding about something. Secretary Fred Korth called them both in and read the riot act to them. As the two admirals were leaving the Secretary's office, Admiral Smedberg was heard to say to Admiral Rickover, "He sure gave us hell, didn't he?" To which Admiral Rickover replied, "Yes, and in your case you deserved it!"

My paper on the Naval Academy leaned heavily on the findings of the Folsom Board chaired by Dr. Richard G. Folsom, President of Rennselaer Polytechnic Institute. The report gave the U. S. Naval Academy a fair wind, noting among other findings that the record of achievement in the Navy of past graduates of the Naval Academy provides evidence that the educational program has been successful in preparing naval officers in the past. Admiral Rickover's attack alleged that the Academy was insisting on developing its midshipmen by traditional processes, processes not designed for the intellectual development required by naval officers who faced modern problems.

I tried to defend the Academy's disciplined approach by pointing to the abilities of the Navy's leaders. A brief excerpt may be of interest:

"In short, while the Navy has and will continue

to adopt insofar as feasible those curricula and educational methods found most productive in other educational endeavors, the military program--call it regimentation if you wish--is not only essential to a successful Navy career, but it is necessary for the development of the whole man. In our opinion, the youth of the nation and the nation itself would benefit by a rejuvenation of more rigorous discipline in its educational processes. In this regard, the Naval Academy will adhere to the traditional processes by which midshipmen are developed mentally, physically, and morally, by which they are imbured with the highest ideals of duty, honor, loyalty, and dedicated service to the Navy and to the nation. It is axiomatic that the future will require of our military leaders more sound and penetrating thought than was needed in any past period. The revisions of curricula and instructional methods already mentioned are designed to foster and to emphasize the foundations required for intellectual development. We would, however, be remiss if we did not rise to the defense of our present naval officers and their intellectual capabilities. We must not allow to remain unrefuted any allegations that our present-day graduates of the Naval Academy have deficient thought processes. We and the nation are well blessed with the presence of our Burkes, Wrights, Booths, Felts,

Hopwoods, Russells, Browns, and Rickovers as living and active examples of the intellectual thinking and decision-making capabilities of Navy leaders. The Radfords, Kings, Halseys, Nimitzes, Spruances, McCains, and Holloways of yesteryear are also among the many outstanding naval leader graduates of the Naval Academy within the recent memory of all of us."

However, the prowess of the USNA was not limited to the creation of great naval leaders. Its influence on civilian education was also noteworthy. In 1960 the Naval Academy graduates included the President of the American Council on Education, the President of Georgia Institute of Technology, the President of the College of William and Mary, the acting President of George Washington University, the Dean of Engineering and Vice President of the Massachusetts Institute of Technology, the President of Rose Polytechnic Institute, and the President of Long Island University.

Furthermore, the fame of Academy graduates as national and world leaders is not limited to the field of education. An abbreviated listing of prominent positions held by Naval Academy graduates in 1960 included the President of General Motors Corporation, the Chairman of the Board of the Texas Company, the President of Standard Oil Company of New Jersey, the Director of Newport News Shipbuilding and Drydock Company, the President of Minneapolis Honeywell Regulator Company, the President of United Aircraft Corporation, Chairman of the Board of Babcock and Wilcox Company, Vice Chairman of the Board of New York Shipbuilding Corporation, Executive Vice President of McGraw-Hill Publishing Company, the Chairman of the Board of Bath Iron Works, President of Radio Marine Corporation of America, President of RCA Communications, President of Atlas Corporation, Senior Vice President of General Dynamics, a famous New York Times columnist, a famous world explorer, and the ambassador to Paraguay.

Despite my effort in defending the Academy's past practices, I feel confident Admiral Rickover's influence was a strong motivation in changing the Academy curriculum to its current structure of offering 26, or is it 28, majors in engineering, science, and the arts in place of the more streamlined traditional curriculum in which all midshipmen with a few elective choices took essentially the same courses.

Here I am in the realm of pure speculation, but it is worth noting that the Academy superintendent who changed the Academy structure to encompass the majors program was Vice Admiral James Calvert, one of Admiral Rickover's most brilliant and aggressive disciples. In all fairness, though, it is essential to note that significant steps had been taken to give emphasis to academic intellectualism in the Academy curriculum before Admiral Calvert arrived on the scene.

Q: Actually, Kauffman did some didn't he?

Mr. K.: The Academic Board as far back as when RAdm Bob McNitt was there as a captain and secretary to the Board had come up with these ideas, but it took time to salt them away.

Admiral Rickover exerted other influences on Navy training. He exercised a strong personal control over the selection of officers who went into nuclear-power programs and he dictated the subject matter they would be taught and the way in which it was taught.

Q: Did this prove disturbing to BuPers--his methods of selecting men for service?

Mr. K.: Yes, it was real disturbing in the sense that you had--the Bureau had to furnish maybe three officers to be interviewed for every one that he picked. This became a rather horrendous situation, trying to find the qualified people that would satisfy him.

Q: In the eyes of the Bureau was it necessary to ask them such searching questions as he has in terms of personal life?

Mr. K.: I think that there were many, including a number of Chiefs of Naval Personnel, who in their minds thought that it was not necessary to be that drastic, but they usually found it advisable to go along with it.

Q: Why?

Mr. K.: Well, I think my story of Admiral Smedberg and Admiral Rickover demonstrates the reason. Admiral Smedberg was one of those scrappers who didn't mind getting into the middle of a fray--but he found after a bit, a considerable bit in his case, that it just didn't pay to argue with Admiral Rickover because sooner or later if he didn't suceed through Navy channels, why, he would be up there telling Congress and the world that those fellows aren't treating me right.

Q: And that, I suspect, is the source of his power?

Mr. K.: This is one of the sources of hiw power. He usually had, whether it was because of the congressional influence or not, the support in the main of the Secretariat. He may not have had complete sympathy from the military organization at all levels at all times, but he got Secretary Korth's support, for example, and he has had the support of other Secretaries over the years.

Nuclear-power schools, for example, were administered and supported by BuPers and now by the Chief of Naval Training. However, when Admiral Rickover was sued by a publisher in a copyright court action, he correctly referred to the Navy's nuclear-power schools as his schools. Some day, hopefully, someone--perhaps one of those young officers Admiral Rickover interviewed and rejected--will write a biography of the Father of Navy Nuclear Power.

I leave my account of his influence at this point, and

hasten on to relate an incident closer to my own interests. One time Admiral Rickover wrote the Chief of Naval Personnel and requested more funding for his nuclear-power training units. He based his increase in requirements on a formula to demonstrate that an increase in student loading deserved a proportionate increase in funding. Even though compliance meant taking many thousands of dollars away from other high-priority programs, the Chief of Naval Personnel complied. A couple of years later, the training load decreased, so I had the temerity to arrange for reducing the Rickover allotment based on a conservative application of his formula by a total of $50,000. Here I learned again that mathematical applications don't always give the right answers. Arithmetic, it seems, is sometimes a one-way street.

While his request for an increase and our later application of a reduction had been formal, polite, and on paper, Admiral Rickover's reaction to the CNP concerning the $50,000-cut was oral, probably not very formal or polite. We restored the $50,000 quick.

Q: Were you present when this came?

Mr. K.: No. I was present when the Chief of Naval Personnel told me to restore the $50,000! We had briefed him on the forthcoming eruption, but that didn't change things--change the way the world went.

I recall one other financial incident. After the budget had been to Congress, Admiral Rickover determined one year that the Atomic Energy Commission was paying more than its share for the Navy's interest in the AEC reactor sites. So he asked for an extra $1,000,000 which was an increase of 100 percent, from BuPers. Vice Admiral Charles K. Duncan had recently then taken over as CNP and he told us that he was confident that he could personnally talk Admiral Rickover out of his demand for the $1,000,000. When he came back from the personal discussion, Charlie Duncan reported to us lesser lights that he had won a great victory. Admiral Rickover had agreed to demand only half a million dollars that year, but would expect the other half as an add-on the following year! With no attempt to be facetious, Admiral Duncan had, in reality, won a major victory!

Two others of my leaders and mentors have now been mentioned--

Q: Before you go on to others, let me ask this question. What do you anticipate when Rickover is no longer on the scene in terms of training and so forth?

Mr. K.: Well, I think the training will continue, and it will continue very much in the same mold as has been adopted and adapted in the past. There may come to be gradual modifications, but he has built up a pretty strong aggregation of many trained nuclear-power experts and officers in the Navy who, in the foreseeable future anyway, I would predict, will carry on pretty much in the same way that he has. I would suspect that the AEC and NavShips would make sure that there is an officer on the staff of the AEC in the same way that Admiral Rickover has been. It's a vital area and a very important area in the Navy. It will become more important, I think, more universal, anyway, as time goes on.

Q: What about his very personal methods of selecting personnel? Will this be used?

Mr. K.: I would look for some modifications in that. I think that sooner or later the selection of personnel to go into the nuclear-power program will come to be very much the same as the selection of people for other very highly important specializations. This is a real personal kind of thing as far as he is concerned and I think as long as he is in the job, he will continue it because he then thinks he can be sure he's got the proper people.

But the selection methods employed by the Bureau of Naval Personnel are not all that bad. The program will continue to get good people even when Admiral Rickover is not in a position to screen them.

Two other leaders and mentors have not been mentioned. These were Vice Admiral W. R. Smedberg III and Admiral C. K. Duncan. They had attributes in common. They were both relatively small in stature, and they both were believers in and fighters for Navy education and training. They were both Chiefs of Naval Personnel. Admiral Smedberg had been Superintendent of the Naval Academy before that time.

Admiral Duncan had had several prior tours in BuPers, one as Assistant Chief for Plans and Policy. My association with each was close and personally rewarding. I accompanied each to numerous sessions in OpNav, OSD, and the Congress, wherein education and training were under attack. They each won my admiration for the manner in which they literally fought to preserve and to improve the Navy's education and training programs.

Q: Why was it under attack from the Congress?

Mr. K.: Not only in the Congress, but in all of these other reviewing agencies. The training organization of the Navy uses more than 20 percent of the entire navy end-strength in terms of students and overhead personnel. Therefore, it stands out as a very vulnerable and large target any time there is any concern about austerity. This, then, becomes one of the places that lots of people delight in throwing daggers at in an effort to reduce it.

Q: It's like the Defense budget!

Mr. K.: It is the Defense budget and training and education, in terms of manpower occupy a real big part of it. Right at the present time, for example, we find the new Director of the office of Management and Budget pointing his finger at education and training in the military services, claiming that it costs 6 billion dollars a year and that this is too big a sum and ought to be reduced.

This kind of thing goes on continually, year after year. Some years you're more immune that you are other years, but this is the kind of thing where you need and enjoy the help and the support of somebody on a high enough level like the Chief of Naval Personnel. They themselves personally entered into the fray and went to the battle grounds, you might say. You were in much better shape than when you were trying to fight a retreating action and didn't have such vigorous support.

Q: And, I suppose, therein lies the major value of your PR efforts under Admiral Yeager and others to--

Mr. K.: Yes, but of course it doesn't take long for people to forget that you have need for a viable training program. Naturally, many people get into the position of having to look for places to curtail. Many times, I'm sure, to people who are in those tough spots, education and training look like a luxury that you shouldn't afford, you shouldn't spend resources on, or at least spend so many resources on.

There's also the problem of misunderstanding. You say, well, 6 billion dollars, that's a lot of money and actually you ought to be able to cut any such sum as that somewhere. But this is before, I think, people have actually looked into where do you cut? When you come to look and see where you could cut, one of the first things that you run into is that you've got programs like the Naval Academy, like the NROTC, like the postgraduate school, like flight training, which are really the backbones of the production of operating personnel in the Navy. There's no way really of chopping substantial amounts out of areas like that, and they eat up a very high proportion of the resources.

Q: These people who take pot shots at the training program and the expense, do they take into consideration simultaneously the complexity of the equipment and the need for highly specialized people to operate these things?

Mr. K.: I don't think there's really any failure on the part of most naval officers, at least, to understand the complexity and the new problems that the equipment have brought, but there is also a matter of being in competition with the operating forces themselves. So you begin to narrow in to the proposition that you're going to have to support the forces afloat, and if you support the forces afloat, something somewhere else has got to give. One of those areas that is attacked most often is training.

In the case of the Congress, I don't believe there's that much attention given to it, but there is—it makes good newspaper reading for congressmen to claim that the Department of Defense and the military in particular are inefficient, don't know how to manage. Therefore, you get attacked more often there on generalities and general principles. They're not specifics of why does it cost this much to train those people? So that there are many instances that come into play insofar as the Congress is concerned that are not necessarily what we would look upon as logical concerns or criticisms, but just--

Q: Political overtones!

Mr. K.: Political overtones that you ought to do better, or different, or somehow it shouldn't cost you so much. They don't really know what you're doing with the money, but you ought to be able to do better with it. Sometimes you get into political overtones like we are at the present time where the Armed Services Committee of the two houses have until this year always given blanket approval to the O and M appropriations without any review. But this year we are being compelled, the Navy as well as the other services, to make a special report to the Congress, which says this is how many people we're going to have in training. The Congressional Committee would like to be in a position to authorize how many people you can put into school.

Now, I'm not sure of my ground in this assertion, but I have a firm conviction that this came about because Chairman Hebert of the House Armed Services Committee has been waging a campaign in the last few years to eliminate defense expenditures at those civilian educational institutions which have thrown recruiters off the campus or thrown NRTOC off.

Q: A kind of a vendetta!

Mr. K.: Right, and he has tried a couple of times to get legislation through that would deny the Department of Defense the authority to spend money at institutions which do not have NROTC units now--that have eliminated ROTC units. He hasn't succeeded in getting that into the legislation, but the compromise appears to be that the armed services committees of the two houses have agreed to require the Department of Defense to set forth what they're going to put in schools.

Q: Is this Chairman Stennis' attitude also?

Mr. K.: I think the Senate really has resisted and this is why Chairman Hebert didn't get his legislation through the way he wanted it--because the Senate was not going along with him entirely. This resulted in the compromise which says "send us a report on what you're going to train."

Q: Hebert's philosophy is in contrast with that which you expressed last time. Yours was a note of optimism for the campuses where the military has been kicked out.

Mr. K.: Yes. I think there's really a dichotomy between the two. I think Chairman Hebert's attitude would be, all right, if those schools want to come back, and they come back on agreeable terms, then, we'll welcome them into the fold. But as long as they refuse to cooperate with the defense interests of the nation either through the recruiting elements or through the training elements, they should not be receiving federal help.

Coming back to Admirals Duncan and Smedberg, it's often been said that BuPers training did not get high-level support over the years, but I can assert from personal observation that when these two gentlemen were in the CNP chair BuPers training got high-level and forceful support.

I had a letter from Admiral Charlie Duncan in December 1972, shortly after he retired from his triple-hatten assignment as CinCLantFlt and so forth--he had two other jobs. It was written in his own handwriting from his retirement haven in Lovettsville, Virginia. At this time, I put aside my usual sense of modesty and quote a couple of sentences:

"Dear Prent,

> If it had not been for wise men such as you to advise me, I could never have survived as Chief of Naval Personnel. I have been very fortunate all of my career in associating with and being helped by fine people."

> This is one of the treasures that I will carry away with me as I depart from thirty ardous years of wrangling, arguing, debating, planning and programming in behalf of Navy education and training."

Q: How gratifying!

Mr. K.: I've got one from Admiral Cagle, and others also,

but I won't quote from too many of them.

There were numerous other talented officers with whom I enjoyed a pleasant, productive, and instructive association. Amont these I would list Rear Admiral Sheldon Kinney, Donald Irvine, Herbert Anderson, and Allen Bergner, all of whom served as Pers C in BuPers for shorter or longer periods. All of these, except Admiral Anderson, have now retired from the Navy, but Admiral Kinney is still immersed in the educational arena as President of New York State Maritime College.

To end this discourse on a personal note may be fitting and proper. I've enjoyed my more than thirty years in the Navy. The Navy's been good to me. But the memories I shall treasure most are the associations, the friendships, and the enthusiasm and dedication of those Navy leaders and colleagues with whom it has been my pleasure and privilege to work. We faced many challenges, frustrations, disappointments, and joy in a few successes. As I fade away, as General Douglas MacArthur said one time regarding old soldiers, from the Navy on 31 March 1973, I will take with me much satisfaction and the recollection that we all labored hard in a dedicated, devoted fashion to make the Navy's training and education system the world's best.

Q: Do you want to quote from Admiral Cagle's letter?

Mr. K.: I had a gratifying letter from Vice Admiral Malcolm Cagle, the Chief of Naval Training, dated the 21st of February 1973;

"Prent,

You will remember that the very first person I even talked to about a new command organization for education and training was you. From that luncheon session you have been my guide and mentor. While we didn't always agree, I found great wisdom and experience in everything you said. It goes without saying that your contributions towards the Navy's training and education goals have been immeasurable."

Q: That, too, is an excellent compliment.

Mr. K.: I'm real proud of these.

Q: Would you cast your mind back over the period that you've been associated with personnel problems and perhaps talk about various tangents which were pursued and which didn't prove to be too fruitful, or shall we say, costly mistakes. Also, more importantly, lessons that can be gleaned from your own experience in this whole area?

Mr. K.: Like most every other thing in the military, a training organization or training program has had its ups and downs. We have operated pretty much in the form of a sine curve in which you may be getting resources in pretty good shape for a while, then things turn around. Most of the difficulties, I would think, that we have experienced have been primarily because there were influences which caused us to go in a prescribed direction. Even though it didn't look as if it might be the right way to go we were forced in that direction at times by circumstances which were beyond the control of our organization.

One example I've already mentioned was the case where we had planned to rebuild a third recruit camp at Bainbridge, Maryland, and were required by political pressures, really, to decide to go in another direction. The total expense that the Navy is going to require in the long run to build a training center at Orlando, Florida, is going to turn out to be considerable.

These are the kinds of things that you continually face. You sort of jiggle from one side to another because of the pressures and do the best you can. But you look back on them and you say to yourself, well, if we had only been allowed to do it this way, then we would have had a better circumstance today than we have. Another example is we wanted to go into Corona--the Naval Hospital at Corona, California, which would have been a good training facility, but we were forced by the politics within the Navy to go into Mare Island where we have a very outstanding facility now. However, the original facilities that were there at Mare Island didn't lend themselves to the same economy as we would have had if we'd been able to employ Corona.

These are the kinds of things that the training manager is continually faced with. We have many times found ourselves in the position of having a deficit of personnel trained in a particular specialty. Then training like mad to build up in that specialty, and then find that some circumstance, either a change in the international situation or some other circumstance, indicates that we trained more than we needed. Then we set about re-training those people that we have trained, so that we can convert them into a specialty that has now become more imperative.

Q: In other words, you're not master of your fate.

Mr. K.: You're not master of your fate. I think the real imperative aspect of managing in this kind of an arena is that the more experience and the more wisdom you can bring to bear, the better the job that can be done in forecasting what the conditions may be, what the changes may come, and then better anticipate what's going to happen.

Another example, is the case of minemen. Right at this particular time it's a subject that's in the newspapers to a large degree as the Navy prepares to remove the mines from Haiphong Harbor. I have experienced times when the Navy practically did away with any experts in the field of mine warfare. One time I remember particularly in which the planners in BuPers decreed that there were enough minemen in the Navy and therefore, we could close down or materially curtail our input of personnel into the mine warfare school. We resisted, and fortunately were on the record with a piece of paper which said, "we think you're going the wrong way here, planners. The outlook is not as bright as you see it. We ought to be keeping a nucleus of capability to train mine men."

It was only a few months after this time when I got called down by the Assistant Chief of Naval Personnel for Plans who said to me, "Why haven't you been putting more people into the mine school?" Fortunately, I was able to go and get the paper that showed why we weren't putting more people in, and the reason was because his people had told us to cut off the flow.

Q: I would gather this was before Korea?

Mr. K.: Right. Then, at that point, we started putting more people into the mine school. So the mine area has had its ups and downs. And obviously, as was noted, right now it's very much in the forefront. It's a real good thing that the mine warfare school continued to operate so that we have somebody in the Navy who knows how to get those mines out of Haiphong Harbor, which are still there today. If it weren't for the training program and the continuation of it, why, the Navy wouldn't have been able to put the mines there in the first place, and they wouldn't know how to get rid of them once they were in place.

These are the kinds of things that are day-to-day or week-to-week situations that you have difficulty in foreseeing. I'm having difficulty in trying to answer your question as to in what way can you avoid these difficulties. I really don't know any way you can avoid them because that's the kind of business we're in. The Navy is supposed to be prepared for the uncertain, or that which is unforeseen. The only answer that I can contrive as a means of combating this unexpected, the ups and downs, and the pressures from outside is that you create and have available a staff which is able to take these things in stride, because of its experience and its knowledge and its brain power.

Q: You're talking about continuity in the staff?

Mr. K.: I'm talking about continuity as one of the ingredients. You need some smart people who have been to sea, who have been in the Navy in operational billets, but you need a combination, I think, of people who are experienced managers. This, of course, can include educators because this is the kind of management business you're in. But you've got to have some people who are able to put two and two together and come up with a reasonable answer as to what will be the best way to proceed under uncertain circumstances.

You may find then that you're overruled by somebody up the line or by some circumstance that gets thrown into the picture. Nevertheless, you will have foreseen to the best of your ability the several ways that it might be possible to go, have chosen the best one that you can foresee, and then have been able to go back to a second best if the circumstances are such that you can't choose the best way.

Q: Now, Prent, you're actually delineating your own experience in recent years, when you were with the organization that you had the perspective and experience.

Mr. K.: Yes. I think though that even back in the World War II days, when we were forming initially the staff, we went out into the civilian economy and brought in people who were in their own element. We grought in many people from many different walks of life--they weren't all school teachers, but there were people from the educational fraternity--there were lawyers and there were people from other walks of life, stockbrokers and people of that type, who were, in the main, real outstanding people in their professions. They, therefore, found it relatively easy to convert their attention to the Navy's problems, the Navy outlook. They had been solving problems of considerable moment in their own fields, so they brought a perspective which the Navy needed real badly, I think at that time. We have succeeded in retaining a good many of the people who came in at that time. To a lesser degree, we have trained some additional younger people--civilians--to take their places in the organization. But I think that if there's one thing that I could offer in the way of advice to people who are going to be following on and required to undertake the problems of the future, it is that you need a staff that has continuity and which possesses some pretty capable management people. This you don't always get in the people who come through the Naval Academy or who are seagoing officers.

Q: Would it help if the Navy developed men for careers in personnel, just as they have done in intelligence and other branches of the service?

Mr. K.: Yes, I think it would. There are steps being taken in the educational field to bring younger people in and train them from the grass roots up to be managers of training enterprises. I am looking forward hopefully to see this program prosper. It does have Admiral Cagle's backing and it may produce what is needed.

Q: This would mean that a man in uniform could go on up the ladder and achieve flag rank in personnel circles?

Mr. K.: Yes, I think this is true under the new system, the new emphasis that the Navy is giving to subspecialties. Personnel management is certainly one of the subspecialties. There are today quite a number of naval officers who have spent many tours in the Bureau of Naval Personnel or in personnel matters. They have become real experts. We haven't had in the training organization yet that kind of continuity in the uniformed service, but we can hopefully look forward to it and strive in that direction, to get people who do stay in the training business. When they come ashore they go to the Naval Academy or the PG school on the staff, or they go to one of the technical training activities. They learn to be training managers.

Then, of course, you need headquarters staff which is

now coming to be concentrated in Pensacola. You need people who are superior in the management field because the capability of the local producers is either made or not made by the people who can get the resources or prescribe the direction of the programs.

I think the most vital staff in the whole Navy is going to become the one at Pensacola. In my estimation, the current staff has potential. It needs further strengthening,--and experience--especially in capability of being able to manage in terms of the total perspective. It needs to be able to see the whole ball of wax, and be able to guide whoever may be in charge in the years to come--guide him in the direction that the Navy might better go, considering all the alternatives that one can foresee.

Q: Now, a personal note, Sir. How do you plan in retirement to utilize your considerable talents and your energies and your great experience?

Mr. K.: I haven't really been advised on this yet. I read a poem that says something to the effect that when you retire you find out that you haven't retired really after all. Your wife has so many things stacked up for you to do that really isn't retirement.

Your question reminds me of what Captain Bob Wheeler, who used to be in Per-C in BuPers, said he planned to do when he retired. He said he was going to go to Pascagoula, Mississippi, and sit in the rocking chair on the front porch and watch the world go by, and then after a year or so he might try rocking a little.

I don't believe Bob really did that and I don't believe I will either. I am more inclined to observe the adage that hangs on Admiral Cagle's Pensacola office wall which says: "Don't hurry, Don't worry. Be sure to smell the flowers along the say."

In any case, as I sit on the Navy sidelines you can be sure I will be watching and cheering for the Navy trainers as they strive toward the world's greatest education and training organization.

Index to

Interviews with

Mr. A. Prent Kenyon

Abbot, RADM James L. (Doc): called from retirement to become Director of Educational Development, 117

Adams, Dr. Arthur S. (Beanie): WW II connection with NROTC program, 156

ADCOP (Associate Degree Completion Program), 107-109

Anderson, Adm. George W.: as CNO not pleased with results of Pride Board - directed study be made for formation of single Navy Training Command, 32; meeting with CNP and others on subject of single training command, 35

Bainbridge, Maryland, Training Center: history of center, 96-97

Baldwin, The Hon. Robert H. B.: Under Secretary of the Navy (1967), instrumental in getting navy to take over training center at Orlando, Florida, 96-97

Beckwith, George: former Navy employee who invented the 'viewgraph' or overhead projector, 129

BOOST (Better Opportunity for Officer Selection and Training), 126

Booz, Frye, Allen and Hamilton: conducts study of Navy training programs and recommends training division in BuPers, 10, 41

BuMed: single exception to Cagle Board reorganization - continues to operate as in the past, 64; 65-67

BuPers: Adm. King puts task of coordinating training under aegis of Bureau, 7; Bureau puts various activities under Fleet Training Commands on Atlantic and Pacific coasts, 9; control of various schools well in hand by 1944, 10; training division in BuPers actually result of study by Booz, Frye, etc., 10; by virtue of CNO directive of Apr. 17, 1964 given responsibility for all naval training except air, medicine, and training afloat, 25; operational training division becomes Functional Training Section, 27; extent of training organization with Bureau as compared with Naval Aviation, 27-28; Hopwood Board recommends (1955) establishment of independent command for Naval Reserve Training, 29; controversy in 1961 with BuWeps over training, 30; see entry under Mason Freeman on reorganization of Pers C, 39-40-41-42; responsibility for creating reorganization fell to BuPers, 43-44; care exercised in getting qualified military for decision points, 44; BuPers writes an instruction on duties of CinCFleets vis-a-vis BuPers for fleet schools ashore, 46; problems that arise as result of this action, 46-47; arranges for Fleet-OpNav-BuPers Conference in Washington, June, 1970, 49-51; account of Washington meeting with Fleet Reps, 52-53; Kenyon chairs meeting to write instruction of Admiral Clarey, 53; Pers C responsible for writing directive to Cagle Board, 59; latest statement on responsibility for training in Navy Regs, 64-65; Kenyon observation that BuPers education and training organization was centrally directed and managed enterprise, 78; overseas indoctrination remains in BuPers after establishment of Chief of Naval Training, 114-115; WW II language schools, 119; use of modern computerized personnel records in making assignments for duty, 124-125; initial responsibility for training and selection of men for Polaris, 149-150; Waves, 188-191; difficulties in dealing with personnel policies of Adm. Rickover, 199-200

Bureau of Navigation, 17

Burke, Adm. Arleigh A.; established Burke Scholarship Program when CNO, 176

BuWeps: in argument with BuPers (1961) over naval training as result of President Kennedy's visit to fleet to witness firing of guided missile, 30

Cagle, VADM Malcolm W.: named by Adm. Zumwalt Chairman of Board to effect a single training command, 59-60; his current effort and task at hand, 77; has taken a great interest in Navy Campus for Achievement program, 117-118; revived Secretary's Advisory Board for Education and Training, 118; quotation from Cagle letter to Kenyon upon his retirement, 210-211; interested in program to bring into Navy young men and train them to be managers of training enterprises, 217; motto over his office door, 219

Cagle Board: commission of this board - not to recommend but to effect a single training command, 58; excerpts from Charter of the Board, 58; Board membership, 59-60; Kenyon voices opinion that civilian influence in reorganized training command has diminished under Cagle, 62-63; work of Committee, 63-64

Cast of Characters: mention of men who have aided development of Naval education and training, 175 ff.

Chief of Naval Training Command: Command set up on August 1, 1971 - result of Cagle Board recommendations, 68; Cagle takes over as Chief with headquarters in Pensacola, 68; responsibility of command, 68-69; reserve training remains outside command for political considerations, 70-71; headquarters will be New Orleans, 71-72; present problems and directions, 77-78; increased costs, 78; need for establishing priorities, 79; CNO instruction on how to establish priorities, 80; see also -

entries under 'problem areas,' 82 ff; discussion of linear planning system, 86-88; Navy uses uniformed instructors largely in teaching efforts, 88-89; construction of suitable facilities, 90 ff; discussion of degrees and granting of them, 100-101; characteristics of Navy education and training, 104 ff; NESEP and its impact, 105-107; ADCOP, 107; correspondence courses, 111-112; educational programs on board U. S. warships, 113-114; overseas indoctrination, 114-115; Navy Campus for Achievement, 116 ff; SABET (Secretary's Advisory Board for Education and Training), 118; tuition and programs, 122-124; efforts to provide educational opportunities to minorities, 125-126; BOOST Program, 126; Pedagogical considerations, 127 ff; use of Viewgraph and closed TV circuits, 130-131; teaching machines, 131-132; use of computers, 131-135; self-paced individualized instruction, 136-140; naval operational Task Analysis Program (NOTAP), 137; roadblocks to use of new equipment, 142-145; no special program for self expression concomitant, with technical training, 145-147; use of models of actual shipboard equipment, 147-148; taken over specialized training and selection of men for duty on Polaris, Poseidon, etc., 150-151; psychological difficulties with Polaris training, 152; early attrition and use of aptitude tests, 153-154; NROTC program, 155 ff; Cast of Characters in Kenyon lexicon of those who have aided Naval education and training, 175 ff.; lessons learned, experience gained through thirty years of work with Naval education and personnel matters, 211 ff.; current thought about special training of men to be managers of training enterprises, 217

Clarey, VADM Bernard A. (Chick): as VCNO signed OpNav instruction outlining responsibilities of CinC Fleets and BuPers for shore training, 49; very much conerned with solution to training problems, 50-52, 55

Classrooms in the Military, Clark and Sloan: published by Teachers' College, Columbia University, 1964, 22; 128-129

CNO (DNET) (Director, Naval Education and Training): headquarters, Washington with Admiral Cagle (1971) as Director: management of education - Naval Academy, Naval War College, P.G. School, NROTC, 68

Computers: use in teaching, 132-136

CotLant: set up by King as fleet training command, 8; BuPers puts various activities under control of this command, 9; threatened elimination in post-war period, 15; name changed to Com TC Atl., 15; 26-27

CotPac: set up by King as a fleet training command, 8; BuPers puts various activities under control of command, 9; threatened elimination in post-war period, 15; 26-27

Defense Language Institute: 119-120

Denfeld, Admiral Louis: DCNO (Manpower), 1946, disagrees with Adm. Radford on Training Policy, 24-25

Dillon Board: presided over by John Dillon, Administrative Assistant to SecNav, 36; recommended new look be taken at reorganization for training after Op-03T had been in existence for one year, 37

Division of Naval Education and Training: focal point of training in OpNav as established by Cagle Board, 67

Dornin, RADM Marshall E.; (Mush), member of the Pride Board (1961), 36

Dubose, Adm. L. T.: Chief of Naval Personnel, 98

Duncan, Adm. Charles: 202-204; quotation from his letter to Prent Kenyon, 209

Fechteler, Adm. William: 26

Freeman, RADM Mason B.: presides over Freeman Board, 33; later as head of Pers C decreed that Pers C should be reorganized in keeping with changes in Weapons Development and coordination, 39; accomplished on basis of weapons systems, types, schools and programs, 40-42

Freeman Board: presided over by Mason Freeman - to make study desired by CNO, 33; recommendations, 34-35; Kenyon is member of this board, 36

Gates, The Hon. Thomas S.: as SecNav fostered Naval Enlisted Scientific Program, 178

General Accounting Office: begins study of Navy's training organization, 48-49; agree with findings as promulgated by OpNav, 49-50

Great Lakes Naval Training Station: 90, 93; installation of shipboard boiler plant for teaching purposes, 147-149

Harbor Defense School: Fisher's Island, N.Y., Kenyon's first Navy assignment in June, 1941; purpose of the school, 3-4; number of students training in 1941-43 period, 4; anecdote involving Adm. Holloway, 180-181

Hebert, The Hon. F. Edward: Chairman of House Armed Services Committee, 168, 171, 207-208

Heyward, RADM A. S. (Sandy), Jr.: Deputy CNP - prevailed in his recommendation that status quo be maintained as result of Op 03T study, 37

Holloway, Adm. James, Jr.: 26; resisted recommendations of Hopwood Board, 1955, 29; anecdote involving Capt. Holloway when he served as Pers C, 180-181, 182-184

Hopwood Board: recommended (1955) drastic change in naval training and this resisted by Adm. Holloway, Chief of Naval Personnel, 29; Kenyon represented position of BuPers before this board, 35

INSGEN: 39 ff.

Jacobs, RADM Randall: Chief of BuPers, 181-182, 187

James, RADM Ralph K.: quoted by Adm. Page Smith, 84

Kenyon, A. Prent: background information, 1-3, 4-6

King, Fleet Admiral E. J.: recognized in 1941 lack of coordination in training, directed cognizance of entire effort be concentrated in BuPers, 7; established COTlant and CotPac, 8; officially establishes (Nov. 1945) the Training Policy Board, 14

Lee, VADM Fitzhugh: at time of Pride Board (1961) felt civilian personnel policies, 32; drew up plan for amalgamating all training under one command, 32; later served in BuPers and came to have closer understanding of Bureau problems with training, 33; 61-63; his attitude towards secular educational standards and those provided by Navy, 73; his concern with need to supplement training of Navy recruits, 75

Linear Planning System: discussion of its advantages and disadvantages as they pertain to training establishment, 86-88

Mine Warfare School: 213-214

M.I.T.: relation of navy program to courses at M.I.T., 103

Naval Air Training: 27; extent of organization and contrast with BuPers, 27-28

Naval Correspondence Course Center: Scotia, New York, 112

Naval Operational Task Analysis Program (NOTAP): 137

Naval Reserve Training: remains outside jurisdiction of Chief of Naval Training Command, 70-71; collaboration between Chief of Naval Training and Chief of Naval Reserve Training, 77

Navy Campus for Achievement: 116; contractual arrangements with U. S. International University, 116-117

Navy Communications Technicians School: move from Imperial Beach, Calif., to Pensacola, 99

Navy Education and Training - characteristics: 104 ff; on the job training, 104, 109-111; need for training as an incentive for re-enlistment, 104-105; correspondence courses, 111-112

Navy Enlisted Scientific Education Program: 105-106

Navy Inspector General: directed to study matter of divided responsibility between CinC Fleets and BuPers for various shore based training schools, 47-48; BuPers role in providing data, 51

Navy Junior ROTC: 168-172. See also entries under NROTC

NAVY REGS: frequency of issue, 26; specific category for BuMed training, 64

Navy Supply Corps School: move from Bayonne, N.J., to Athens, Ga., 97-99

NESEP Program: quotation from House of Representatives Report, 1957 - DOD appropriation bill, 185-187

U.S. NEW HAMPSHIRE: Stationary Training Ship - based at Newport, R.I., late 19th century, 17

Nimitz, Fleet Admiral Chester W.: as CNO (1946) issued directive on naval training responsibilities, 25 -26

NOTAP - Naval Operational Task Analysis Program: 137

NROTC: first established in 1926, 21; in 1971 comes under direction of CNO (DNET), 68; 155 ff.; summary of early efforts, 155; Holloway Plan, 155-156; contribution of Dr. Arthur Adams, 156-157; use of quota system with colleges and universities, 159-160; problems with Ivy League schools, 161-163; recent trend to locate new units in black universities and militarily oriented schools, 165; Stearns-Eisenhower Board, 167-168; Navy Junior ROTC, 168-172; reluctance on part of Navy to set up unit at the Citadel, 173; present appropriations for institutions where NROTC units have been eliminated, 208

Operational Training: a special division of Navy Training as recommended by Booz, Frye, etc., 11; specialized training for radar, communications, etc., 11-12; becomes functional training section, 1946, 27

Orlando Navy Recruit Training Center: 93-94, 97; described by Clark and Sloan in Classrooms in the Military as an "almost fantastic institution," 129

Pedagogical Considerations - present day training: 127 ff; (see entries under Chief of Naval Training).

PG School, Monterey, Calif.: story of how move was made from Annapolis, Md., during Korean conflict, 90-93; current problems of the school, 121

Pride, Adm. A. M. - Chairman of the Pride Board: established to deal with conflict over training between BuWeps and BuPers, 30 ff.

Pride Board: presided over by Adm. Alfred M. Pride, established to study personnel training conflict between BuWeps and BuPers, 30; membership of Board, 31; 32-33; Kenyon appears for BuPers before Board, 35

Priorities: See entries under Chief of Naval Training Command.

Public School Education vs. Navy Education: 72-74

Raborn, VADM W. F., Jr.: witness before Pride Board (1961), 31; 150

Radford, Admiral Arthur: as DCNO (Air) in 1946 opposes proposals of BuPers for Navy Training organization, 24; as result Adm. Sprague, DCNO for Personnel (1946) presents directive to define responsibilities for naval training - this issued by Adm. Nimitz, CNO, 25, 27; quotation from his with emphasis on training, 179

U. S. RICHMOND: Stationary Training Ship - replaces NEW HAMPSHIRE in 1890, 17

Rickover, VADM Hyman: his influence on Navy Education, 193-194; story of Rickover and Smedberg, 195; Kenyon writes a defense of the Rickover criticisms - quotation from his paper, 195-199; some sources of power, 200; funding for his nuclear power training units, 201-203

Rosenberg, David: promoted through BuPers the subject of overseas indoctrination, 114

Ruckner, RADM E. A. (Count): was Op-03 T at time study made on possible reorganization of training set up, 37

SCPTR: Standing Committee for Personnel Training and Readiness - established in Op 03, 28

Sikes, The Hon. Robert L. F.: instrumental in getting Navy to move
   CT school from California to Pensacola, 99

Smedberg, VADM William R., III: 203-204

Smith, Adm. Harold Page: as CinCLantFleet - quotation from him on
   training problems, 83-84; 179

Sprague, Adm. Thomas L.: draws up directive later issued by CNO
   (Apr. 17, 1946) on responsibilities for Naval Training, 25-26

Stearns-Eisenhower Board: reported in 1950 on future of officer-
   candidate education in armed services, 167-168

Strean, VADM Bernard M.: as CNATRA saw Naval air training as a
   "loosely decentralized" one, 78

Stroop, VADM P. D.: adviser to Pride Board, 31

The Formative Years: section of memoir containing review of early
   history of training in U. S. Navy, 16-24; period - 1890-1920,
   17-18; naval education and training in several wars, 19; quality
   of enlistments in 1930s, 19; WW II, 21-22

The Goerge Washington University: educators on staff have trained some
   of Navy experts, 74, 100-102

Towner, RADM George C. (Bull): 91

Training Policy Board, office of CNO: 5-6; Kenyon's experience in
   BuPers during WW II pointed up lack of coordination in training
   facilities, 6; comes into being as a board due to recommendations from BuPers in Oct. 1945, 13-14; officially established
   by Adm. King on Nov. 16, 1945, 14; BuPers plans vigorously
   opposed by Adm. Radford and BuAir (1946), 24; gradual diminution of authority, 27

Training Problem Areas: technological breakthroughs provide major hurdle for service training program, 82-85

Tunney, Gene: became head of Physical Training Section of BuPers – reorganization in WW II, 41

Tyree, VADM John: member of Pride Board (1961), 36

U. S. Naval Academy: begun in 1845, 16; in 1971 comes under CNO (DNET) in Washington, 68; building program in last 25 years, 93; forerunner in use of computers for teaching purposes, 132-133; Kenyon writes paper on curriculum and teaching efforts at Academy – to refute charges of Adm. Rickover, 194-198.

U. S. Naval War College: begun in 1881, 16; comes under CNO (DNET), 68; engaged in conducting Correspondence Courses, 112

University of Rochester: provides course in 'defense systems management,' 102

Vinson, The Hon. Carl: guides Navy to the purchase of buildings and space, Univ. of Georgia, Athens, Ga., for a new Supply Corps School, 97-99

WAVES: 188-189

Weakley, RADM Charles E.: BuPers helped him form a DD school at Newport, 177; nature of course provided there, 177-178

Withington, RADM F. S.: members of Pride Board, 1961, 31

Wright, Admiral Jerauld: first senior member of Training Policy Board (1945), 14

Yeager, RADM Howard (Red): 184-185; his assistance to Naval Enlisted Scientific Education Program, 185-186, 191

www.ingramcontent.com/pod-product-compliance
Lightning Source LLC
Chambersburg PA
CBHW080614170426
43209CB00007B/1428